Inspired

Inspired

The
SECRET
of BOB
PROCTOR

by LINDA PROCTOR

BURMANBOOKS

Cover design: Lloyd Arbour, LifeSuccess Publishing
Text design: Jack Steiner

Distribution:
Trumedia Group
c/o Ingram Publisher Services
14 Ingram Blvd.
LaVergne, TN 37086

ISBN 978-1-8974042-2-5

Printed in Canada

To Marguerite Proctor (Feb. 27, 1913–Sept. 30, 2006)
Mother of Helen, Bob and Allan
This book is possible because of her!

Contents

Foreword

Bob Proctor, like the title of his first book, has totally manifested: *You Were BORN RICH!!!*

His riches take many forms. Bob has abundance of all things: ownership of his own mind and spirit, money, family, friendship, fame, ideas, wisdom, contribution, service, thoughtfulness, books, movies, audios, and a legacy that will last forever.

This book of loving, vivid and thoughtful attributions stands as a testament and legacy to the great work of a great and thoughtful man. It is a powerful statement to be well loved and thought of by an extended family and a worldwide group of friends. Bob is universally loved, respected, admired and appreciated for his consistent, insistent and persistent desire to share the truth principles, philosophy, and practices with millions of people everywhere.

It has been my privilege to be Bob's friend and colleague for over twenty-five years. I have owned two businesses with him. Bob stimulated us to be exceedingly challenged, grow and become MORE. Our goal was to help individuals to say yes and self-create wealth. Those with the real aspiration, dedication, and willing perspiration to get to high, lofty and inspired destinations did and some still are becoming millionaires and multi-millionaires.

Building people and expanding their dreams is Bob's genius and mastery. Bob introduces students to themselves, their minds and the enormous potential that each and every one of us has. I have watched Bob speak well over a hundred times and listened many more times on audio and CD and on my iPod; and I have always learned more and come to understand the great truths and principles infinitely better. I am deeply thankful to his commitment to excellence and his deep and fervent desire to be of ever greater service to others.

I have witnessed Bob's ascent from the corporate stage to the world stage. While he is seventy-five years young, I acknowledge, as he does, he is just beginning. Bob sees there is so much to do and he desperately wants to do it all to make the world infinitely better off.

I am thankful to call Bob a great friend and super world server.

Happy reading of this heart touching and soul penetrating book. It will profoundly influence you, your lifestyle, fortune and future.

Mark Victor Hansen

Introduction

By Linda Proctor, wife of Bob Proctor

He loves to ballroom dance, is a romantic who writes beautiful notes and adores all creatures from insects to dogs.

These are just a few traits of my husband of 26 years that most people don't know about. Inside this book, you'll learn much more about Bob through the eyes of his family. The man we know as the teacher of life also has had a profound impact on those closest to him.

The book you hold in your hand was conceived as a living tribute to Bob, for his 75th birthday. It soon became apparent, however, that it was more than that....much, much more. As I gathered stories, I began to realize they were life lessons relevant to all of us, right now, today.

The stories are real. They are small windows into the past. These memories have been written by Bob's children, grandchildren, nieces, nephews, brother, sister, aunt, uncle, cousins and in-laws. They tell a story of the very powerful, positive influence that Bob has had in their lives. Many of them are successful entrepreneurs; one is a Superior Court Judge. The youngest are just beginning to distinguish themselves in sports, the arts and academics.

I met Bob Proctor 30 years ago in a seminar in Atlanta, Georgia. I was a 27-year-old widow struggling as a sales representative in the insurance industry wanting—needing—better results. After that seminar, my sales results improved dramatically—going from

$25,000 a year to just under $500,000 in a very short span. Bob believed in me right from the start. He saw my potential. I rose to that expectation. In fact, he was the first person who believed in me, outside the non-traditional path that a woman in the '70s was supposed to be taking.

We shared many, many dinners together. In the beginning I was unsure if Bob was working with me because the company that hired me (and for whom Bob was working) had a goal to hire and promote more females, or if he had a personal interest in me. Every dinner the discussion was about me. I continued to go out to dinner with him. Then one night, I looked at him and realized I was in love. This was a man who thought differently than anybody.

A couple of years ago, after appearing in the movie, *The Secret*, Bob Proctor was introduced to the world. Suddenly, after 40 years of working diligently with individuals and corporations around the globe, leading them to great improvements in their results, Bob had become an "overnight" sensation!

Bob's friends and family couldn't be more delighted, but none of us were surprised. Having been steadfast in his work, his goals, his ideals, throughout most of his life, Bob is a rock to all those fortunate enough to find themselves in his circle. Friends and family know if they need advice they can go to Bob; ironically he won't give you any. Instead Bob will do what he does best—he will ask you questions which will help you solve your own dilemma. He uses the people closest to him as his sounding board, but never asks them to make a decision for him.

This book is being compiled at a time when the media is relentlessly churning out news story after news story that paints a grim picture of our economy. Many comparisons are being drawn between these troubling economic times and the Great Depression—the very era Bob was born into.

And yet Bob achieved success without the benefit of education, money or family connections. He leads by example and reminds us that no matter what our current situation may be, if we have the will, determination and the relevant knowledge to change it, we can and will—and dramatically.

Marguerite, Bob's beloved late mother, had a tremendous influence on Bob, his brother Allan and his sister, Helen. Even today, in their 70s, at an age when many face retirement, they remain active and relevant in their respective businesses. These dynamic siblings show no sign of slowing down, and their commitment and excitement in business, remains steadfast and strong. Clearly, their shared environment played a significant role in shaping their character.

By taking and combining the common sense life lessons Bob learned from his mother, along with the knowledge that he extracted from years and years of self-driven study, Bob has created life-altering seminars and powerful speeches. He has changed so many lives, but remember, it started with his own. Because he was able to so dramatically improve his own results, he has dedicated his life to sharing that experience, and helping others do the same.

We frequently hear of people being referred to as, "go getters." Bob has always encouraged everyone to be, "go givers." And what a world it would be if we all practiced this philosophy! Bob is truly all about helping the people who come into his life, both personally or professionally.

"The geniuses of the world are dead...but in their day... they were considered heretics."—Bob Proctor

The jury is still out on whether Bob is a genius. But as you read this book, you will clearly see that, for much of his life, Bob's path has been different, and one of his own choosing. That path has been a challenge at times; but it took him a vast distance, from his humble beginnings, to places he could never have imagined way back when. And now, you will hear how he has shared the benefits of his strength and courage—to be different, to make his own way—with his large and loving family.

Few people are able to see the extremely soft and gentle side of Bob that we as a family know. Bob is known as the strong, confident man on the stage who passionately speaks about his beliefs. At home, Bob has a rule that no insect be stepped on—a spider on the floor must be picked up gently in a Kleenex and placed outside.

To further understand Bob, listen to what his grandchildren tease him with: That he "is a child trapped in an older person's body." At 75 he displays incredibly "young" interests and excitement. He has an amazing attitude toward everything. This attitude has been nurtured over and over again. Bob continues today to be a serious student of what he teaches and loves. He has a voracious appetite for reading and his library is growing faster than we can catalogue the books that he reads.

I can't tell you how many times we have watched the movies *Lawrence of Arabia* and *Patton*. To Bob, the lead roles in these movies didn't just act, they became their characters. It's a model Bob teaches people around the world—act the way you want to become and you will become it.

Through his teachings, Bob inspires people to achieve more, and to pursue their most cherished dreams. Through his actions, as these stories reveal, he inspires us all to become better people. I hope you will see that Bob walks the walk just as much as he talks the talk.

Inside this book, you will see some cherished family photos. We are a close family, and very proud of each other. There is a space to insert your own picture alongside ours. If your environment is not conducive to being your best, just put your picture here, with us, and visualize the environment necessary to realize your path to success and fulfillment!

My hope is that you will use these stories as an inspiration to be the best you can be. I can think of no better role model than my husband, Bob Proctor. I have always known what a wonderful person he is; after reading this book, you'll understand why. When you find yourself faced with important decisions, or facing difficult challenges, read a lesson in this book and then ask yourself, "What would Bob say to me now?"

Linda Proctor

Inspired

Your Picture here

Forgetting the Basics

RAYMOND PROCTOR
—Son

It was one week before Christmas in 2001. My son Benjamin was five years old at the time. He seemed healthy, but he had large lumps on the side of his neck; the doctor had been running blood and ultrasound tests on them, trying to determine a diagnosis. I was on a morning commuter train heading downtown for a rather important meeting about a company merger that had just been announced. My wife Toni called on my cell. I could tell immediately something was wrong. The doctor, not the doctor's office, had called. He needed to see both of us immediately. He would not tell Toni why. We both started thinking the worst.

As soon as I was off the train I arranged for a rental car and headed straight back home. Toni and I met at the doctor's office within an hour of the phone call. He informed us that Sick Kids Hospital in Toronto did not have any available beds. He had already made arrangements for us to attend a similar hospital in Kingston. This was two hours east of us. He informed us they had a concern that Ben had lymphoma. We would be meeting a pediatric oncologist in Kingston and we should pack for staying overnight. We walked out of the doctor's office and to our separate cars to head home and pack.

Dad and Linda had been making arrangements to purchase our family a membership at a private alpine ski club as a Christmas present. The first thing I thought of was the need to call them and tell them not to. We wouldn't be available to go skiing this year due to the news about Ben. I called and Linda answered the phone.

I remember sitting in this unknown car and the emotion of the moment hitting me like a brick wall. I told Linda the news and told her to cancel the ski membership plans. Shortly after I hung up with Linda, Dad phoned me back. He was compassionate but firm. He told me they were going ahead with the membership and for me to get my thinking straight. He said Ben is fine and not to give energy to any thought but that. He had been teaching me that my whole life, but it can be so easy to forget in the moment. He was even more emphatic that we not show any emotional weakness in front of Ben. The last thing we should do was to make him fearful.

We arrived at the Kingston hospital and as we walked through the front doors the doctor came up to us and asked if we were the Proctors. My immediate thought was "it's bad." When do you ever get greeted like that at a hospital? I stopped my thought and pictured Ben healthy and skiing. Ben had a CT scan that evening then a biopsy the next morning. We waited patiently for the results from the pathologist. They came back negative for cancer. We were incredibly relieved and exhausted. The entire experience left me in awe as to the personal character of the pediatric nurses. What incredible interpersonal skills they have to do what they do every day. Dad's words, of putting my thoughts on the right track, were all the easier with the wonderful support of the nursing staff.

I realized that day the importance of positive thinking. Whether or not it made a difference in my son's diagnosis I will never truly know. However, I know it made a difference for my son. Being strong for Ben allowed me to properly address my concerns for his well being. My first thought had been one of emotion and worry. Imagine the damaging impression I would have made on Ben, had I expressed my fear and worry in front of him. Those emotions really would not have been about his well being, but my own. If I had taken a moment to reflect, I would have realized that positive thoughts and attitude are the only things that would express my concern for his well being. I appreciate the fact that Dad called back that day to remind me what I needed to do: Think positive.

Five days later we had the most grateful Christmas we had ever had and started skiing as a family the next week. We ski as a family today.

It's Just a Piece of Tin

BRIAN PROCTOR
— Son

For as long as I can remember, Dad had a saying that, to my adolescent mind, seemed rather strange. He would say, "Either you own the car or the car owns you." To make that point, he would refer to people who buy a really nice car, but won't let anyone drive it - including those closest to them (I think we all know some of those people). They pamper the car more than they pamper the important people in their lives—and sometimes even themselves.

Little did I know at the time that a lesson Dad taught me when I was 17 would be a lesson I would teach my own son, 29 years later.

In 1976, Cadillac was producing "the last convertible". It was the beautiful, heart-stopping, powerful Eldorado. I remember vividly the day Dad drove that car into our driveway. It had a shining white exterior, with tan, ultra-soft leather. It seemed to silently glide into the drive. It looked enormous, even for the days of the giant gas guzzlers. I still remember the smell of the new interior, and the huge smile on Dad's face, as if it were yesterday.

I always loved driving that beautiful car. I learned to drive in it. I got my license in it. As far as cars go, it was "my first love."

Back then, like today, my father travelled a lot. He was—and still is—on the road more than he is home. When I was younger, this could be a big perk, because—yes, you guessed it—he would freely leave his car for me and my cousins. We all got to enjoy that very special vehicle while he was away.

During one of his trips, I got into a pretty serious accident. I drove into the back of another vehicle—it was completely my fault. I remember looking at the damage to the front of Dad's car, and feeling dread, sorrow and then fear, at having to tell him what I had done. I had no idea how my father would react, but my imagination took worry and fear to new heights.

It took awhile, but I mustered up the courage to call Dad. I told him the whole story—how it was my fault. I described the damage that his beautiful Eldorado had suffered.

I will NEVER forget the concern and the peacefulness in his voice, as he asked me, "Brian, are you ok? That's all that matters. The car is just a piece of tin. It can be fixed." Then he said, "It's called an accident because that is what it is. You didn't intentionally go out to wreck the car, so don't let it bother you another moment."

The car was repaired, and life went on. The next time Dad went out of town, I got to use the car again, without hesitation. Dad loved that car, but he didn't let it control him. This is a lesson I carry to this day.

How lessons can come back around in the strangest ways.

I am often asked what it's like to have Bob Proctor as a father. For a presentation to a large audience, I decided to incorporate a story about my dad, and I chose to tell the story of the Eldorado, because I really wanted everyone to understand what a great man my Dad truly is. It was fun reliving it, and I enjoyed the story as much as everyone else in the group.

Ironically, the very next day, I got a call from my son saying that he had wrecked my truck.

I could hear the worry in his voice. I believe I responded, word for word, exactly as my father had, 29 years earlier. I know my voice was also calm and peaceful; Danny hadn't been hurt, and that was truly the only important thing—not the piece of tin.

The Simple Things

TONI PROCTOR
—Daughter-in-law

Bob appreciates the simple things in life while staying focused on his mission.

The backyard of Bob and Linda's house is the setting where we come together every summer to celebrate Bob's birthday. Bob and Linda have created a little piece of heaven in the heart of the city. There are huge mature trees of every kind all around, small flowering bushes and even a tree that blooms with red roses. The local squirrels are well fed, the local chick-a-dees are cared for, and the girls, "Miss Honey and Missy Love", the Pomeranians, are always perched on a lap, included as a part of the family. The grandkids, and sometimes the kids, swim. I must say the energy is quite calming.

After a day of swimming, eating, and talking, we bring out the cake to sing "Happy Birthday Dear Grandpa." After the cake and ice cream are enjoyed Bob is presented with presents of all shapes and sizes. Bob does not want for anything, so what do you give a man who has everything his heart desires?

I really learned something about Bob one year. It was his 69th birthday; as always Bob had been travelling and teaching. Ray (my husband and Bob's son) had suggested a wireless mouse for his Dad, because he spends a lot of time in his office, or on the plane, with his computer and he loves gadgets. (The first person I have ever known to have an iPhone was Bob.) As an accessory to his new mouse, we thought we would give him a personalized mouse pad. First Bob opened the wireless mouse and then the mouse pad. His face lit up, and he showed it to everyone. It was the pad that really made an impression with him; it was imprinted with a photo of all of his grandchildren taken poolside one summer afternoon. Bob thanked everyone for their gifts, and I noticed that he went directly to his office, which overlooks the backyard, and put his new mouse pad beside his computer.

Bob works diligently to achieve his goals, and is living the life of choice. It is the simple things that he truly appreciates. We all want the luxuries of life. They can make you quite comfortable. Bob is surrounded with luxury and I am sure he finds comfort in it. However, that is not what makes him happy.

Other stories in this book speak to his generosity. Bob can easily part with his possessions, as he owns them, they don't own him. His happiness comes from appreciating his friends and family. The day he opened this simple present I saw with greater clarity the old adage of money doesn't buy you happiness…love does. It is food for the soul.

The Terror Barrier

LINDA PROCTOR
— Wife

Bob and I met in one of his seminars. Following that seminar my income jumped from $25,000 a year to just under $500,000 in a very short period of time.

Bob later told me that I was one of his best students; but I have to admit, I was motivated to impress him! Bob continued to mentor me and I really came into my own as a salesperson.

Several years later Bob suggested I should start my own financial services company. The thought of owning my own business appealed to me but I certainly didn't have the knowledge or skills required to run a business. I proceeded anyway assuming that because I was competent in sales and reasonably competent in sales management, it would not be that big of a stretch to run a business! Oh, my gosh! What was I thinking?

Well, it wasn't long before the responsibilities of running the business—bringing in the clients and the revenue required each month—overwhelmed me. On this particular day, I left the office early and went home. I just wanted to crawl in bed and pull the covers over my head…which I did, really!

Sometime later Bob came home and asked what I was doing in bed. I told him I was over my head with my business and wasn't sure I could keep going. He looked me in the eye and very compassionately told me that he loved me but that I had two options:

That I could quit and he would support me or;
I could continue on and he would mentor me.

Now, that wasn't what I wanted him to say. I wanted him to tell me that he would step in, do it for me, and then when things were running more smoothly I could take over again. I quickly realized that was not an option in Bob's mind.

Well, I didn't want to quit...I didn't want to stay home and be supported but I clearly didn't believe I could move forward either. Bob talks about the terror barrier...well I was there and it was paralyzing me! I could either let fear push me back to a place I did not want to be or I could move forward, breaking new ground into growth!

I laid in bed, first feeling sorry for myself and then getting a little agitated with Bob for not doing it for me. The more I thought about Bob's response of quitting, the more riled I became! I finally jumped out of bed determined to figure things out and make it work....with Bob's mentoring!

Bob has always been supportive and has encouraged me to be the best I could be. However, he has never done the work for me, nor has he done it for anyone else for that matter. I know now that had Bob done the work for me, I never would have gained the confidence, knowledge and skills I needed to run and grow a business.

Years later Bob admitted that it was hard for him to watch me struggle with something that would have been so easy for him to do. But he understood that it was a struggle I had to make to grow into the person I needed to be, to truly run a successful business.

When you find yourself at that terror barrier, find someone who can help you refocus on your goals and support you through this challenge to move forward toward your goals! It is definitely worth the struggle. I can't imagine the person I would be today had I chosen to retreat to what appeared then to be "safety"!

"There should be at least three cardinal rules for success in personal achievement, whatever the field may be:

(1) Complete passionate devotion to whatever field you have chosen.

(2) The need to concentrate, to the exclusion of all else, when working on, thinking about, or executing whatever discipline you have chosen.

(3) An utter pitiless sense of self-criticism, far greater than that which any outsider could give."

—Isaac Stern, violinist

The Little Black Dot

TJ MOIR
—Cousin

Many years ago, Bob and I were in a beautiful hotel in Kuala Lumpur, Malaysia. This particular day, Bob was very low key. I never thought I'd see it, but it appeared that Bob actually had nothing to do.

That morning, we had breakfast and took a walk down this neat little jungle street to find the monkeys. I remember how confidently he walked down that street even knowing that the monkeys had a reputation for jumping out of the trees attacking people. I have a picture with Bob carrying a stick. It was a really cool time.

I was there playing the Asian golf tour, and I told Bob that my game was kind of stuck; it just didn't seem to be getting any better. Well, of course the first thing coming out of Bob's mouth was. "It's your attitude, your concentration!" I responded "No, it's my grip or my balance or some other golf mechanic."

Bob grabbed his pen (nice pen, by the way) and walked over to the wall. He drew a little black dot. "Now TJ," he says, "I want you to stare at that dot and really focus on that dot." I recall his voice and how committed he was at getting the lesson across.

He continued: "Now, every time your focus shifts from that little black dot, I want you to become aware that your focus has shifted and immediately go back to concentrating on that dot and nothing else."

My objective was to increase the time that I was able to focus only on that dot. Sounds easy, but it's not. Try it. The floor creaks, the phone rings—endless possible distractions. Bob was teaching me to focus on the task, not become distracted by the details that were drawing my attention away from it. I'm happy to say that my mental skills did improve with this exercise, and so did my golf game.

It's Not About Me!

CURTIS PROCTOR
—Grandson (14)

I love my Grandpa. He is always interested in me and what I am up to. I do not live very close to him and he travels a lot. But, when I see him, he always asks me what I am up to. By asking me questions about myself, Grandpa makes me feel important.

My Grandpa has a genuine interest in other people's achievements. I have been to his seminars; I have seen him working. He has become successful helping other people.

I have a paper route. When I started as a paper boy I had 32 customers on the street that I live on. Delivering the papers is the easy part of the job. I get home from school, have a snack, and three days a week get to stuff advertisement flyers into my papers. On average there are 17 flyers for each paper. It takes a long time to stuff 32 papers with 17 flyers each. I then deliver in rain, sleet, snow, hail or shine. I do all of this and my customers do not have to pay. It is a voluntary payment. Collection period is every three weeks. I write out my list of customers, I put on my change pouch and I head out the door to collect.

Like Grandpa, when I knock on my customer's door, I ask about them. Every collection period, I learn a little bit more. I learn about their pets, I learn about the boat in their driveway, and I learn about their hobbies. I ask questions.

Each time I collect from them I'll ask a question about something we discussed before. I think they appreciate that I am interested in them.

My Mom tells me that some of her friends' kids have paper routes and only get paid 50 percent of the time. Of all of the customers I have, only two or three do not pay.

I think that my Grandpa knows best. Being genuinely interested in others makes you more successful in what you do.

Always Give Your Best

LINDA PROCTOR
—Wife

After almost 50 years giving speeches, lectures, seminars, writing books and articles, you would think Bob wouldn't need much preparation for his presentations anymore. And that probably is true; but Bob is the consummate professional, always preparing and always giving each audience his absolute best. It's true, he could give some of his lectures and seminars in his sleep—but he never, ever does. Every time, after all these years, he gives it his all.

At 75, Bob is very healthy; his doctor tells him he's his hero, with his stamina and energy. But one day in Toronto, Bob was very sick with Salmonella poisoning. He had a high fever and could barely move. He had been in bed for days. He had a two-hour lecture to deliver late in the day, and we all encouraged Bob not to go; it would be too demanding, too hard on him, given how sick and weak he was.

But of course, he would have none of that. So our plan then was to get everything set up so that Bob could go in at the last minute, have very little contact with anyone, and at the very end, whisk him out of the auditorium and back to his bed.

As I sat in the audience, watching, I was amazed. He was entertaining, animated, and of course, he made all his points clearly and forcefully, to help the audience and the company that hired him.

He drew on energy that no-one in his office thought he would have. That audience got the very best of what he had that day, and I'm sure no one even suspected he was not well.

At the end of the seminar, Bob was backstage. He wanted to sit down before going to the car—he was exhausted. Some people made their way backstage, and asked him to autograph a few books—which he did without complaint. He was soaking wet from the fever and was leaning against the wall for support. Staff hurried to find him a chair. Before they could find one, he slowly started to slide down the wall toward the floor. We ran to grab him so that he wouldn't hurt himself. He was truly spent—there was no more energy. He had given everything he had to that audience.

I've heard Bob say many times "a pro is at their best regardless." Pros don't make excuses—they focus their mind on the task at hand and do the work to the best of their ability, every day. On that day, that point was really driven home.

Don't Take It Personally

LEANNE PROCTOR
—Granddaughter (Age 17)

In the modeling world, you get a lot of rejection! When I first started modeling about 4 years ago, I would go to auditions and if I didn't make one (there were many I didn't make), I would ponder for days and days, 'What did I do wrong?' 'Why didn't they like me?' 'Was I not nice enough?' My feelings would drive me crazy and made me even more nervous for the next audition.

During the summer of 2006, I went to New York for a 7-day modeling competition. The first few days were the competing days. The last day was a callback day, where agents from around the world would get to meet the models they felt had a lot of potential.

A few weeks before I left for New York, I was with my Grandpa explaining to him my nervousness about the competition; it was really an audition for hundreds of important agents. I explained to him how I got upset and didn't understand when I didn't get a job I really wanted.

He asked me questions like, "Did you do your best? Did you feel good about your audition? Did you understand their direction and were you able to follow it?" The answers to these questions and others were all yes, and they really helped me understand why I didn't make the auditions.

The reason was simple: they just didn't want the look I had.

It had nothing to do with how I presented myself; they were just searching for a different look!

Now, when I go on auditions, there are still some that I don't make. But I now know that I am in charge of my self-image and I never take it personally. Thanks Grandpa!

The Strangest Secret

BEVERLY PROCTOR
—Sister-in-law

I was a healthy woman most of my life. So when a bad cough was diagnosed as pneumonia, it never occurred to me that anything could be seriously wrong. Two rounds of antibiotics later, I wasn't any better. The doctor suggested I should go to the hospital for x-rays.

At the hospital I was told that I needed further tests and to have my husband bring what was necessary for a two-day stay. Impossible! I had three small children and a kennel full of show dogs. Nevertheless, I had a four-hour time frame to get back to the hospital.

I knew my mother would stay with the children for a few days, and my 'doggie' friends offered to take care of the kennel, so I packed a small bag, and my husband Allan and I left for the hospital.

Little did I know that I would not return home for six weeks. There were lots of tests, all of which were painful and frightening, and many discussions over whether or not to operate and remove whatever was causing the cough.

Finally a decision was made and a date was set to operate, May 24, 1970.

After the surgery, Allan and Bob met one of the doctors as he came off the elevator.

"Your wife has six months to live."

Al fainted. This is where Bob stepped in. He insisted that the negative doctor be removed from my case and that the operating surgeon would never tell me I had cancer or that I had only six months to live.

Bob visited regularly. He would set up a tape recorder and I listened to Earl Nightingale's *The Strangest Secret* over and over again, telling me that "whatever I could conceive and believe, I could achieve." I admit that most of the time I was too medicated to really listen, but it was there, in my subconscious.

I believe one of the reasons I survived lung cancer during a period when no one survived lung cancer, not even my father or John Wayne, was because Bob eliminated any opportunity of negative thoughts being introduced to me. He forcefully created an environment that consisted of only positive thoughts. I don't even want to consider what my mind would have done had the doctor been permitted to advise me of his opinion. Bob truly understands the power of positive thinking.

I never knew I had cancer until many months after they had removed the tumor and part of my lung. I never conceived and believed I had cancer, and so I never achieved cancer. I never had any fear of dying. I never thought about Allan having to deal with my death and raising three young children on his own.

The Strangest Secret works whether you want to accentuate the positive, or eliminate the negative. I've heard my case was written up in the medical journals as a miracle. I guess you could call it a positive miracle.

Social Knowledge

RAYMOND PROCTOR
—Son

High school and I did not see eye to eye—it wanted from me what I did not want to give. Initially I thought that perhaps I was attending the "wrong" school, so I changed schools. My marks got better, but I was soon back to square one. Then I decided that school itself, was not for me, and so I relieved myself of the burden of high school. I can only imagine today the concern and frustration that this action caused my father. Though he tried to direct me back to school, he ultimately allowed me to find my own way.

Shortly after dropping out, I began to question my decision. Dad must have sensed this, because he and Linda began suggesting that I consider enrolling in a university in Florida. They were clearly trying to appeal to my love of the south, hoping that the prospect of a tropical climate would lure me back into school. It was a nice try, and I did visit a university campus in Florida, and was intrigued, but somehow I just wasn't motivated enough. It wasn't until I travelled with a friend of mine, to visit her sister at a university a couple of hours from Toronto, that I bonded with the idea of going to university. And to accomplish this, I would need to return to high school and get my diploma—which I did.

Throughout high school my marks were never particularly good, so I was concerned as to whether or not I would be able to make it at university. When I shared this with my Dad, he responded, "Don't worry about the academic knowledge, go for the social knowledge." He elaborated further, but those words are what stuck with me. And from that moment onward, I developed a new perspective on going to university.

Frosh week came, and I focused on being "social." In subsequent years I volunteered to help run Frosh Week, and was always a part of one club or another. An odd symptom of all this social activity was that I began to enjoy university in general, and it reflected in my grades. By the time I graduated, I had obtained as much social knowledge as I had academic knowledge.

To this day I use the knowledge of working and interacting with people that I gained from my experience on campus, far more than I use the academic knowledge. Dad understands people and human behavior and he understood the hidden value that I would gain from attending university. Clearly the reason for doing something is not always visible. Sometimes there is more hidden value, than in the direct apparent benefit, of whatever you are doing.

Visualization

PIXIE LOW
—Sister-in-law

Children might be too young to read or write, but even the very young can set goals. Bob suggested to me that for children, visualization was one of the key steps. So instead of writing down their goals, my small children would play the movie in their mind of the things they wanted or wanted to achieve.

It was the summer before my youngest child Alexis turned 8. Her birthday is in September, and she—like every child I know—wanted something and didn't want to wait to have it for her birthday. She wanted a "car" for her fashion doll. The car was huge and space was an issue but it was also expensive. I explained to her that this would definitely have to wait two months until her birthday. We had a few battles over it until she decided to set a goal.

She knew that if she played the "movie in her mind of the things she wants," you somehow get them quicker.

So we set the goal. September 5: One large pink fashion doll car.

Our first step was to "make the movie."

I asked her questions that were similar in nature to questions Bob had asked me about my goals, questions such as:

➤ Do you know where the car will stay in your room? Yes, she said, she could see it.

➤ Do you see yourself playing with the car? Yes, she said, she could see it.

➤ Do you see yourself getting the car and unwrapping it for your birthday? Yes, she said.

➤ Are you having fun when you think about the car? Again, yes.

And on it went until she could play the questions back and see it as a movie in her mind.

Every day for the next six weeks, I would ask her about the car. She would tell me in detail about playing with it. She loved the car she didn't have yet.

Well, it was finally time to make her birthday wish list. I had already decided that I was going to give her the car and was going to scratch it off her list. But to my surprise—and no, it wasn't because the list was two pages—there was NO car.

Holy moly! That's all the child talked about the entire summer! I went right away to find out. "What gives?" I asked her. "I thought you really wanted the car!"

Her reply was simple. "No, I don't want it any more. I played with it enough." Hearing Lexi say those words struck me as to the true power of visualization, just as Bob teaches it. Here was a little girl, eight years old, who had mastered the technique so well that she became bored with a toy she never had.

It became so clear the power she will have, to focus on goals, as she grows up. However, it struck me even more that I too have that power, and can use it the same way Lexi did to focus on my goals and lock in on my desires.

When I told Bob this story he agreed Lexi has certainly grasped the important step of visualization.

"You make the world a better place by making yourself a better person."

—Scott Sorrell

Everyone Can Change

LINDA PROCTOR
—Wife

Back in the 1960s, when Bob's results started changing dramatically, he became almost like a missionary—wanting to help everyone experience the radical, positive change he had brought about in his own life. Once a month, he would travel to the Kingston Penitentiary, a maximum security prison several hours from home. He made arrangements with the prison that he would work with anyone who wanted to attend his sessions. As enticements, he brought donuts, coffee and cigarettes and so he always had a number of inmates show up for his workshops.

There was one in particular, named Joe, who was allowed out of solitary confinement for his sessions. Bob said he clearly came just for the cigarettes, donuts and coffee. Until Joe, Bob had never seen anyone smoking, eating, drinking and talking at the same time. Joe was a disruption, not interested in the session or what Bob had to say—just the goodies on offer.

Bob knew he had to do something about his disruptive influence; but he also knew that Joe was serving time for armed robbery, and that he had shot someone in a hold-up. Bob said that he mustered all the courage within himself to confront Joe for the sake of the class. Bob went toe to toe with Joe, later admitting that he truly thought he might end up getting socked in the face. Nonetheless, he steeled himself: He told Joe that he was "an idiot"

(I believe the language I heard was the non-child version). He told him that he could earn more than Joe could steal. When the session was over, Joe was headed back to solitary confinement, and Bob was leaving for home. Bob made him an offer. "I must know something you don't; if you listen, I'll teach you."

Well, Joe didn't punch Bob. In fact, Bob said that Joe laughed and said "Okay." After that, Joe really did listen. He became one of Bob's biggest supporters in the prison, paying attention and really investing himself in each and every session. And when Joe was released on parole, he went to work for Bob, becoming one of his best employees.

I didn't know Joe at the time; this was all before Bob and I met. But I did get to know Joe, even though he had moved on from working for Bob. Joe never went back to prison; instead he built a decent, fulfilling life for himself and his family.

Years later, when Joe passed away, one of the first calls his wife made was to Bob. Joe's change was dramatic, and permanent. There were only winners because of Joe's change!

My results changed dramatically as well after meeting Bob. My self-confidence surged. My income skyrocketed. And of course, I came to know true love!

Looking back I realize that Bob believed in me. I didn't have confidence in my own abilities at that time, but I believed in Bob's belief in me. Like Joe, my change had a ripple effect on all those around me. Find someone who believes in you and lock into that to make the changes in your life! Everyone around you will benefit!

We Become What We Think About

MARGARET MOIR
—Aunt

It is devastating to visit your doctor and be given a life-altering diagnosis about the state of your health. My story begins when I lost all sensation in my legs and was diagnosed with Multiple Sclerosis. Having young children to raise, this was one of the most challenging things that happened in my life. I can tell you the look and feel of that wheelchair was not something that I welcomed.

Many family members arrived at my home to express their concerns, and rallied to help with the children. Bob and I have always been very close. When he asked what was wrong, I painfully expressed that I had been diagnosed by my doctor with MS; I told him that I had been told I would never walk again.

Bob asked me point blank, "Why would you accept their prognosis?" He then caused me to question the prognosis from the doctors by reminding me of one of his favorite quotes; "we become what we think about." It was a quote taken from Earl Nightingale's *The Strangest Secret*. And I would come back to it over and over again. Yes, it was obvious that I couldn't walk, but what "if" I could beat the odds? What if I could find a way to contribute to the raising of my children?

Bob would visit with me almost weekly, motivating me and building my determination to walk again with his positive messages.

I remember my first attempts to walk again. I would literally crawl up the sides of the walls, falling down, over and over again, until I learned to stand on my own. I never regained the feelings in my legs—but I was able to walk again, raise my children and lead a normal life.

This was more than 40 years ago. Just before Christmas of 2008, I had some tests done to evaluate the progression of the MS. Modern technology being what it is, the doctors informed me that I did not have MS, and I replied: I knew that!

Bob would never encourage me or anyone to ignore medicine or medical treatment, but he did encourage me not to accept or believe a negative prognosis. He taught me that I become what I think about; I decided my prognosis and made it my only thought. I listened to Bob and I became what I thought. I have lived a long, full, normal life. I will soon be 80 years young and I can't imagine what my life would have been like if I had not listened to Bob.

Get Your Head in the Right Place

COLLEEN FILICETTI
—Daughter

In the mid 1980s I was going to university in Illinois, majoring in Dance and my family was living in Toronto, Ontario. It was about a 12-hour drive home. You couldn't just decide to come home for a weekend.

During the first semester of my senior year, I got very sick. I ended up in the hospital for a short time, and was told that in order for me to regain my health I was not to participate in any of my practical classes for the next two months.

Doing this would mean losing my semester, which in turn meant I would not be able to graduate that year.

I was sitting in my dorm room feeling very alone and very discouraged, and I turned to my Dad for a 'pep talk.' I wasn't able to go see him, so I did the next best thing and phoned him. I explained to him that I was going to lose my semester; that I wouldn't graduate.

"Whoever said you will lose the semester?" he said. "The doctor didn't say you couldn't go to class, he said you couldn't participate." I didn't think he understood what I was telling him. I explained I could still go to my academic and theory classes; I had no issue with those credits. It was my practical classes I would be unable to complete.

I was wrong. He did understand. He said I was in negative place and I had to get my head out of it. I had to focus on healing, and in order to do that, I had to stay positive.

He repeated himself, saying that even though I couldn't participate, I could go to class. He said, "Watch the teacher, watch the students and do everything that they are doing—in your head. Your mind doesn't know any different. As far as it's concerned, you're still dancing."

After he said that to me, my attitude completely changed. Having Bob as my father, I knew exactly what he was saying to me; I guess I just needed to be reminded.

I went to class everyday and participated—mentally. When I was given the okay from my doctor, I was able to do all that I had missed. My muscles were sore, but my body knew what to do. I did complete my semester and in turn graduated with Honors that same year.

Even though I was raised in a "you can do, have or be anything you want" household, there are times when I allow myself to become a victim of circumstance. I find comfort in knowing my dad is just a phone call away.

Respect

BENJAMIN PROCTOR
    —Grandson (Age 12)

One time when we were at Grandpa's house I was following my cousin Danny around. We went into the kitchen where Grandpa was. Danny and Grandpa started talking. I don't remember everything they said, but I do remember them talking about respect. Grandpa was explaining that it is important to like yourself. He talked about respecting other people, but he also talked about respecting yourself. He said it is easier to get friends if you treat people with respect.

I thought about the friendships I have. I realized I have some good friends because I like them and treat them with respect. I also realized that I have lost some friends because I didn't treat them with respect. I like myself and feel good about my friends, but I don't like myself when I think about the friends that I have lost. I realize that people will often treat you the way that you treat them.

Grandpa has met many people in his life. He has so many friends that he has filled a cruise ship twice with people that like him. I know Grandpa treats people with respect and I want to have as many friends as Grandpa has one day.

"Faith is the bird that feels the light and sings when the dawn is still dark.

—Rabindranath Tagore

Faith in You

RAYMOND PROCTOR
  —Son

Although the passing of my father's mother, my Nan, was expected, the grief was still a lot to handle. The entire family had time to prepare for the inevitable, as well as the opportunity to say good-bye. However, the actuality of what was to come was far more than I had imagined it would be.

Nan was the pinnacle of all our families. Her attitude and energy meant so much to everyone. I, my wife Toni, and our three boys would make an annual April trip to spend two weeks with Nan in her Florida home. I made this trip regularly with friends and cousins even before I was married. I had nearly 25 years of visiting Nan in Florida. From day one, all of her neighbors and the extended community would always say how great they thought she was. This praise grew stronger as she climbed in age.

All of her direct family travelled to Florida to celebrate her 90th birthday. There was a big party with well over 100 people. The sincere recognition by everyone as to her incredible character was testament to how we felt about her. A simple example of this character was the fact the she played 18 holes of golf the day before her 90th—and even made par on a few holes! Impressive, but even more so, when you are aware that she was nearly blind, due to macular degeneration. She only had limited peripheral vision. This feat was possible because she was unlimited in attitude.

Imagine the weight I felt when Dad called me after Nan's passing and asked me if I would do the opening speech at her memorial service. He shared that he, his sister and brother all agreed that they thought I was the best one for this huge responsibility. They wanted me to set the tone and the pace for the service.

I am not known for being the most talkative or outgoing when it comes to my family. I was not sure why Dad, Helen and Al all thought I was best for the opening speech. Dad said they all had faith in me. I wasn't sure I held the same faith. First, I had no idea how to pay tribute to such an incredible person. Second, I had no idea how I would keep myself composed. I questioned Dad a few times on whether or not they were sure it was me they wanted. Dad indicated that they would understand if I declined, but he assured me they had faith that I was the right one for the job.

I found my own space and time to reflect on what I could say. The most consistent word I could think of to describe what everyone felt for Nan was "admiration." I surrounded that word with my speech. Every sentence started with "admiration," then followed with a description of her admirable character.

My speech was prepared, but that was only half of my challenge. Composure was left to be tackled. Moments before the service, I was in a hallway off to the side of the pulpit, mentally preparing for opening the service. I was working hard to contain my emotions. My nephew Danny passed by, gave me a hug to say hi, and asked how I was doing. I couldn't speak: I was too choked up. How was I going to speak in front of hundreds of people, if I couldn't speak to one? I breathed deeply and tried to take my thoughts elsewhere. They had faith in me. I wanted to meet their faith.

I walked up behind the pulpit and started to speak. I was aware of Dad, Aunt Helen and Uncle Al all in the front row. I looked out over top of them rather then at them and simply felt their presence. I wanted to do right by them and their mother. I started to speak and continued through my message while only having my voice crack once while saying goodbye to Nan.

Having unconditional faith in others when they don't necessarily have it in themselves is a strength that can lift others to greater heights. The number of compliments I received after the service was heart warming, but not as much as the faith I received from Dad, Helen and Al.

Putting faith in others has been a cornerstone of my Dad's character for the better part of his life. Without it he would not be half the man everyone knows him to be. One ingredient of being great is making sure you make other people feel great first.

*"Patience and perseverance have a
magical effect before which difficulties
disappear and obstacles vanish."*
—John Quincy Adams

Angel Food Cake

MORGAN FILICETTI
— Granddaughter (Age 14)

It was soon going to be my 10th birthday. When Grandpa asked what I wanted, I told him I wanted him to teach me how to make his famous Angel Food cake. I couldn't ever remember seeing Grandpa cook but I remember my mom saying that Grandpa used to make amazing Angel Food cakes. I usually only get to see Grandpa with my family; I thought this would be the perfect opportunity to spend time with him alone. Grandpa said he'd love to teach me.

The day of my birthday, I went to Grandpa's house. Even though he had just returned home from overseas and must have been very tired, he kept his promise.

He had enough ingredients to make three cakes! Grandpa explained to me that when he was taught how to make an Angel Food cake, he first watched and took notes, then he participated in making the second and the third one he made by himself. Because he was taught this way he has never forgotten how to do it. He said he was going teach me the same way. I was going to observe him, participate with him and then do it all by myself.

Grandpa was very patient with me. Each cake took approximately a dozen egg whites and he soon realized when it was my turn to participate, he had to go and buy more eggs because I wasn't very good at the separating part. He never made me feel bad; he just said we needed to get more eggs and practice a bit more.

When it was my turn to do it by myself, Grandpa said I did a great job. He always makes you feel good about yourself. We brought the cakes to my birthday party and everyone enjoyed eating them!

When teaching someone something new, you have to be patient and calm. My Grandpa is a good teacher. When I help out with the little kids at my school, I try to be just like my Grandpa was with me, patient and calm.

I really enjoyed my time alone with Grandpa. Even though he is very busy, traveling all over the world, he always makes time for things that really matter... like family.

(See Grandpa's Angel Food Cake recipe on page 138.)

Practice Mentally

COLLEEN FILICETTI
—Daughter

Everyone remembers going for their driving test. Not everyone remembers failing it. I do. I was devastated.

Dad sat me down and said it was a good thing. A good thing? How can failure be a good thing? He was very quick to correct me: I didn't fail; I just didn't get it yet. I needed more practice.

In our house, practice didn't mean only physically doing it; it also meant mentally doing it. We learned it was necessary to do both.

Dad had me close my eyes and practice parking the car. He talked me through every detail just as if I was actually physically parking the car; from opening the car door, turning on the ignition, driving to the parking spot, putting the car in reverse, parking it, turning off the car and getting out. He went over that with me several times.

He said, now that you've made the movie, play it over and over again until you have it mastered.

Dad always had us visualize; he said our mind is unable to differentiate between what's real and what's imagined. If we play that movie in our mind over and over, and practice mentally, it will become fixed in our mind.

Dad said visualization is a very powerful tool: You must always keep your mind focused on the positive, because what you see you will be.

And the next test? I passed, of course!

Hearing and Listening

CHRISTINE FILICETTI
—Granddaughter (15)

During summer vacation we often go to Grandpa and Grandma Linda's house. It is one of my favorite places to spend my time. They have a beautiful backyard with a pool. It is so calm and relaxing.

When I was younger, most of my day was spent in the pool, only taking time out to eat. Grandpa always keeps his pool nice and warm so we never get cold. He would come in and out of his office or sit in his "outdoor office" and cheer us on as we swam and dove off the diving board. As I got older though, I spent less time in the pool. It was more fun for me to sit around the table with Grandpa and talk. We have great conversations. He is always interested in what I have to say.

I sometimes bring one or two of my closest friends with me. What I admire a lot about Grandpa is that he really takes the time to learn about my friends and their interests. He's never one just to say "hi". He's taught me the importance of asking people about themselves, and not just talking about oneself.

What I love the most about Grandpa is that he taught me that all people are important and have a voice, no matter how different they may be. He also taught me a valuable lesson—the major difference between hearing someone and listening. If you hear someone, you are just letting the words come into your mind, float around for a while and disappear after a short period of time, not even remembering what they said. It doesn't make them feel important. But, if you really listen to a person, their stories will sink into you…you are involved in what they have to say. Everyone feels important when we listen to them.

Circumstances

ALLAN PROCTOR
  —Brother

I have often said that our mother gave us our work ethic, but Bob showed us how to use it. For that, I am forever grateful.

One of my favorite memories, one that motivates me whenever I'm in a difficult situation, took place in the early 1970s while I was working with Bob in the seminar business.

These were early days in the self development industry—days when positive thinking and personal development were not something to which many people gave much thought or credence. In general, people blamed everything that was wrong with their lives on the circumstances and their environment (some things never change).

We were promoting Bob's seminars by having a free one-hour preview.

On one particular day, a principal from IBM was going to be attending. Of course, we were excited about the possibility of working with that company. Creating a favorable impression was always important, but on that day, we were especially attentive.

The room was set up, and another associate and I were ready to greet the attendees. The IBM rep arrived early, so we entertained him while we waited for the others to arrive. As the time to start got closer and closer I realized that no one else was coming. Cold panic set in.

When Bob entered the room, there were only three people there—me and two others. Bob could have chosen to walk away and quit, but he stepped up behind the podium, and presented the program as if the room was full!

I still can't begin to imagine how difficult this was for Bob. But not only was he effective that day, he went on to work with IBM on a number of occasions over the years.

I've often wondered where he would be today if he had chosen to be defeated by an empty room. I really believe Bob moved to a higher level that night in the 1970s.

The lesson I learned, almost 40 years ago, was never to quit, and never to blame your circumstances.

The Math Mark

COLLEEN FILICETTI
—Daughter

As a teenager Dad never told me what to do, but he was always there for advice. He was very good at being objective, and he always helped me to see how my choices would have an impact on how I handled situations in the future—but ultimately, the decision was mine to make.

A prime example was when I was in my last year of high school. I was doing poorly in Functions. I wasn't failing, but my grade was not one to be proud of. I wanted to drop it—it was dragging down my overall average. I went to Dad to talk to him about what I was considering, to see what he thought.

Now, Dad is not a man of many words when you ask his advice; rather he listens, really listens, to what you have to say. Then he'll ask a couple of questions, and before you know it, the answer is staring you in the face.

He asked what I had done to try and improve the mark. I told him what I thought was a good answer. But as soon as it came out of my mouth, I knew it wasn't. Dad looked at me and suggested that before I make my decision, I should find the person in my class who had the highest mark and ask if he/she would tutor me. I told him I would.

I left the room thinking, "How am I going to go up to someone I had never really spoken with and ask him for help?" I was nervous.

The next day in class, I went to Rob, the star math student, and told him I wasn't doing very well in class, and asked if he would be willing to help me. Much to my surprise, he said he would. I look back now and think it must have made him feel really good to have someone come to him for help.

Rob spent his lunches with me in the library. He was so patient, going over the formulas again and again until the light bulb went on!

I not only earned a good mark, but I learned something much more valuable: Don't quit when things get tough—rather, seek out those with the expertise to help.

THE SECRET OF BOB PROCTOR

Calmness from Repetition

RAYMOND PROCTOR
—Son

About a year ago I was sharing with Dad how I was worrying and stressing over business. He told me not to worry. I thought to myself, "That's easy for you to say." He explained further; he said not worrying wasn't the same as ignoring or not caring about the situation, quite the opposite. "You should be consciously concerned about it," he said. "But worrying is something completely different."

"Calmness of mind is one of the beautiful jewels of wisdom." This is the first sentence of the last chapter, Serenity, in *As a Man Thinketh* by James Allen. Dad suggested that I write this chapter out in long hand then read it aloud a couple of times a day every day for at least 90 days. It felt a little odd writing the chapter out and reading it aloud, but I thought I may as well, it wasn't going to do me any harm.

If you have never read the chapter, you should. Dad has developed an incredible ability to remain calm and serene in the face of great adversity. This is a characteristic and skill that I'm sure he acquired over time as a result of diligent study and practice.

I learned a lot about the power of calmness from this exercise, but it was his method of teaching that taught me something else. Dad often tells someone to do something specific every day for at least 90 days. Most people do not follow this advice. I don't always follow this advice! It can seem odd and even become boring, listening or reading the same thing so repetitively. Dad stresses that repetition is necessary in order to change our thoughts or paradigms.

Reading the chapter every day for over a month became an exercise of near mindless repetition. I could almost recite the chapter without reading it. I thought I understood everything it was telling me. Then one day the words in one paragraph painted a much clearer picture in my mind. Initially I understood the message on an intellectual level; suddenly I was aware I now had it on an emotional level.

Dad's technique of teaching me about the power of calmness gave me an even greater understanding of why he stresses the importance of repetition. In order to change a characteristic or habit, your change has to make it to the emotional level.

Setting Goals

BRIAN PROCTOR
—Son

I have always understood the importance of se[...] think my father had instilled that in me from the time I [was] a young boy. I can't begin to count the number of times in my life that Dad has asked me, "What is your goal, Brian?"

A few years ago, I was a bit lost and struggling in my work. I was really unhappy and didn't know what to do. I knew that going to my father for advice would help.

If you know my father at all, you know that he can be very direct. The last thing he does is 'beat around the bush.' Within minutes of our meeting he very matter-of-factly said, "Brian, you don't have a goal." I think I came up with some lame excuse and said that I did. But I didn't present a very good case, and in no time at all had to agree with him.

He then proceeded to have me write down on a piece of paper all the things that I either wanted to have, do or be. He said to write it all down no matter how ridiculous it may seem or how impossible it may be to achieve. After some time I had a pretty good list. Dad had me go over that list and talk about each item. I think he could hear in my voice when I had a passion for something or not. He then had me cross out some of the items that did not mean as much to me.

going over it several times there was one thing that really stood out: A brand new, customized Harley-Davidson motorcycle. At the time, it really was a ridiculous thing to go for based on obligations I had with my young children, finances and my business. But Dad said it didn't need to make sense to anyone else; it only had to make sense to me. If it inspired me to do things that I might not normally do, if I didn't have it as a goal, then it would be a good thing. He then had me make a list of all the things I needed to do to accomplish that specific goal. I was not to focus on what wouldn't work—just on what would.

I remember walking away with a newfound passion for life. I wrote my goal down on a card and carried it with me in my pocket so that I would always be thinking of it. I got pictures of it, framed them, and placed them on my desk.

I don't remember how long it took, but I did achieve my goal. From that point forward whenever it comes to setting a new goal, I go through that same exercise. It has never failed me.

The Hourglass

DAN PROCTOR
— Grandson (Age 19)

Grandma Linda and Grandpa always had hourglasses in their house; for some reason, it didn't occur to me to ask why until I was 18. When I did ask, Grandpa picked one up and began talking to me about life and how the sands passing through it symbolize our time here on earth.

"We know what happened yesterday, and the days before that," he said, pointing to the bottom of the glass, filling up with sand. "We also know what is happening right now." He pointed to the waist at the center of the hourglass. "The thing we don't know is this part," he said, as he pointed to the top, which still contained the bulk of the sand.

"We don't know how much sand is left so we should realize that the past is not our concern; neither is the future set in stone." Grandpa said that most people spend too much time reliving the past or worrying about the future. We should enjoy every second for every grain of sand we are given, regardless of our age or our present life circumstances. The present is all we are guaranteed and we should enjoy it.

I believe that living each moment fully and seeing the good in everything that happens is what Grandpa teaches and lives.

*"The purpose of human life is to serve
and to show compassion and the will
to help others."*

—Albert Schweitzer

Family First

HELEN BRINDLEY
—Sister

Marguerite Proctor, our mother, was an incredible individual and role model not only for her children but for her grandchildren and great grandchildren. She was an amazing lady with unbelievable stamina! She lived in her own apartment right up to the end of her life.

Marguerite absolutely loved life. In her later years she would laugh and say, "I can't believe all my kids are in their 70s." Frankly, we couldn't believe it either—especially since we are all still working in our own businesses!

The last six months of her life was a time none of us will ever forget. Even at the end, she never ceased being interested in what everyone was involved in—her children, their spouses, her grandchildren and friends.

We were all busy but were able to work out our schedules so that we were able to take turns being with her every day until she left us for a higher realm.

Bob was very busy at this point, but put his life on hold to spend time with our mother. When Bob would come through the door at Mom's apartment she would lighten up and say, "Here's Bobby!"

Bob would make her lunch or a cup of tea and sit with her to chat. She just loved Bob being there; he would joke with her, wash up the dishes and make her comfortable. Sometimes he would bring butter tarts, which they both enjoyed so much, and say, "I know we shouldn't be eating these, but isn't it fun, Mom?"

Bob was not just putting in time with mother—he was really involved in her life. Right up to the end, she knew she was loved and remained an important part of all of our lives.

It was wonderful to see this very successful man, my brother, drop out of his enormously busy professional life to focus on being a caring son. His actions demonstrate that no matter how busy you are or how important your work may be, you always need to be mindful of the true value of life and what really matters. Bob knew that at this time, being a son was far more important than being a teacher. And it was this way until mom left us.

Keep Your Eye on Your Goal

PIXIE LOW
          —Sister-in-law

My children, Matthew, Mackenzie and Alexis, have grown up in an open-minded, "anything is possible" environment. Thanks to Uncle Bob's influence, they are goal setters. Bob has taught them, when they are setting a goal, to focus only on the end result.

While Matthew was in the 4th grade he was taking martial arts, and was soon to take a particular test that would see him advance to the next belt level. So attaining that belt became his goal.

One day before the test, Matthew hurt himself during recess at school. He could stand, but moving his hip joint was painful. An x-ray showed nothing serious, but the doctor advised him to stay off of it.

The next day, Matthew insisted that he wanted to take the test. We thought he was joking, knowing that breaking two boards, with both feet—in mid-air—was a requirement—and Matthew could barely walk up the stairs. But he suited up and we went to the arena.

During the first part of the test, the Master would call on a student. The child would jump up and say "yes sir!" Then they would then perform their routine and go back to their seat. When it was Matthew's turn, he could barely get up. The Master told him that he could not be given any special consideration; he suggested he take the test at a later date. Matthew wouldn't hear of it. He performed the first part of the routine. When he was done, he took his seat.

For the final part of the test, each student had two chances to break two boards with both feet, in midair. When Matthew's turn came up, the Master again asked him to take the test at a later date. Matthew thanked him, but said he would continue. On his first attempt, Matthew broke only one board and could barely stand up. Matthew retreated back to the starting position. He paused and stood looking straight at the boards.

I thought he was reconsidering, when suddenly—Matthew took off! The room was filled first with the sound of one crack and then the second crack. Matthew took his seat until each student finished the test.

At the end of the test, the Master asked Matthew, in front of everyone, how he was able to do what appeared impossible. (And remember, Matthew was a 4th Grader at this time) Matthew's reply was very simple. "All I could see were the boards breaking."

Matthew had applied what Uncle Bob had taught him. He set the goal, and focused entirely on the end result.

You Were Born Rich

LINDA PROCTOR
   —Wife

Born Rich was Bob's first book. But the version you may have looks nothing like his first draft—believe me!

It was in early 1980. Bob had been on the road for a couple of days. He had started writing *Born Rich*—in long hand. This was before personal computers. He could have used a Dictaphone, but Bob has always found it very convenient to work on planes and in taxis, so everything was handwritten.

When he got home from that trip, he told me that he had finished a good bit of the book. He was really pleased. He reached for the folder; he wanted to read some of his recent chapters to me. Only the manuscript wasn't there—he had left it in the back of the taxi!

I was in complete panic mode. Bob couldn't remember the name of the taxi company. The folder containing his precious manuscript didn't have his contact information on it; finding it seemed hopeless. Nevertheless, I called every taxi company I could find in the phone book, trying to locate all of his hard work.

But what I couldn't believe is how calm Bob was. At one point, he told me that it was okay—that obviously that version was not meant to go to press, that he could and should do it over, and better.

Most people in situations like that would be angry, quit, or worse yet, misdirect their frustration and anger at something or someone else. Not Bob.

We never did locate that folder, and Bob did rewrite the book. Looking back, I believe that if Bob had finished that original manuscript, he would not have done as much with it. By the time he finished the next version, he had re-established his business after moving from the US to Canada, and had a bigger base of clients to offer it to. The timing, it turned out, was perfect.

Looking back it's easy to see that what seemed awful at the time was in fact a really great thing! But we never would have realized it if Bob hadn't managed to be so calm in the first place. It was a potent lesson: You'll always have setbacks. To get where you want to go, you have to get back up and push forward toward your objective—no matter what.

Overwhelmed? Put it on Paper

RAYMOND PROCTOR
—Son

There was a time when I was getting overwhelmed with all of my responsibilities; I found it hard to accomplish anything. My fear was paralyzing me, keeping me from being able to make decisions or execute. When my appetite and sleep were also being affected, I realized I needed help.

I considered calling Dad. That's not always the easiest decision, because Dad usually delivers some stark reality, and the simplicity of the perspective he provides can leave you feeling silly sometimes for having had the thought or feeling that caused the call for help in the first place. So I braced myself, and picked up the phone.

What surprised me was how brief the call was. Dad asked what was overwhelming me. "I don't know - everything!" I said. He told me to write it down on paper and then call him back to discuss it. He was gone before either one of us could really even say goodbye. When Dad is done talking, he's done.

I sat there perplexed, still holding the phone; then I put it back in its cradle. I had been expecting—and prepared for—a rugged mental adjustment. Instead I got a thirty-second call without even a goodbye!

I decided it best to do what he suggested; so that I could get the help I was looking for. I began to write out the things that were causing my fear and anxiety. I was surprised that there were not nearly as many issues as my feelings led me to believe. Putting things down on paper added simplicity and clarity to what was concerning me. Before I even called my father back, I was already feeling more in control. I found I was able to start listing points of action that I could take to address some of my concerns.

I did call my father back, and shared with him my surprise— the list was so small and simple! He laughed, and with his calm understanding, he told me that whenever he starts feeling like he is not on top of things, he goes through the same exercise himself.

I find myself putting pen to paper more often now; it keeps me right on top.

Good Thoughts to Feel Good

GIANCARLO FILICETTI
—Grandson (Age 9)

When I was eight, my Grandma Antoinette was in the hospital. I was sad because she was very sick. My sisters and I stayed at my Grandpa and Grandma Linda's house for a few days because my Dad and Mom wanted to be with her.

I was cuddling with Grandpa on the couch and he was watching golf. I was pretty upset so he stopped watching golf and talked to me. He asked me to tell him how I was feeling. He told me to stop thinking about her sick in the hospital. He said to think of all the good times that I had with her. He asked me questions about all the fun times I had with my Grandma, and remembering those times made me smile.

Grandpa taught me not to think about all the negative things, and that I should only think of positive things. Sometimes it is hard, but there are always ways to do that and when you do, you feel good!

"Take the first step in faith. You don't have to see the whole staircase, just take the first step."

—Martin Luther King Jr.

Higher Image

TONI PROCTOR
—Daughter-in-law

My mother Pat introduced me to Bob when I was a teenager, more than 30 years ago. Bob was holding seminars on a regular basis in Toronto. One evening after a seminar, Pat and her husband John invited Bob for a coffee in the hotel restaurant. They had already started to develop a friendship. They wanted to ask Bob for some advice on how to achieve a big dream that they shared. This big dream made them feel uncomfortable; they were unsure of their goal, and how to achieve it. Bob, as always, took time from his busy schedule to coach them.

At the time we were living in a small two-bedroom basement apartment. It was early November, and their goal was to be in their first house by Christmas. This was a big goal—Christmas was less than two months away! The biggest obstacle most people face in getting their first home is accumulating the money. Both Mom and John worked in commissioned sales. Therefore, earning large sums of money in a short period was not out of the question. But their sales were down and they were afraid—afraid of many things, but they were also very dissatisfied with their current circumstances.

I wasn't in their meeting with Bob, but I'm sure that it wasn't an easy conversation for them. However, they followed Bob's direction and trusted in the logic of what he had to say. Although I was only a teenager, I noticed that my Mom and John's demeanor changed. They were happy, almost excited. They had moved into action focusing on the goal. They were busy, but it was a good busy. Every evening the conversation focused on the progress that they achieved that day. They were focused on the higher image of their dream, in spite of living in a basement apartment, as a reminder of their past results.

Mom and John achieved their goal! We had Christmas dinner in our new house. We didn't have much furniture, but one piece I remember was the dining room table Bob brought over so that we could have that special dinner as a family. We stayed in that house for a number of years. Mom and John continued to set goals. Many of those goals focused on significant renovations to the house to make it even more of a home.

As a young girl, I really had no clue how important this experience was for my Mom and John. As a parent and homeowner today, I look back on their goal with greater appreciation and understanding of what they achieved. You can change your circumstances and accomplish great things in a short period of time. In order to achieve your heart's desire, you must stay focused on the higher image, not the lower concern.

The Magic Within

DAN PROCTOR
—Grandson (Age 19)

Magic has always fascinated me. At 16, I started learning magic tricks, and the first person I performed a trick for was my Grandpa. What did he do? He pulled a silk scarf out of his pocket and then made it instantly vanish right in front of my eyes. Then, he did it again. I was totally awestruck. Until then, I never knew that Grandpa liked magic too!

Grandpa always seemed to know how each trick worked. He knew exactly where I had gone wrong when I messed up but he always encouraged me to never give up and to keep practicing until I mastered each new trick.

I think about my magic all the time. I'm always turning coins or cards through my fingers. I know that I must bug everyone around me—they seem to know my magic tricks as well as I do!

I have heard Grandpa talk about falling in love with what you do. I love my magic and practicing for me is fun. I guess that's good. I love practicing because I have also heard Grandpa tell people that they need to practice over 10,000 hours to truly master anything. He said that most people stop practicing or studying something as soon as they can do it—when in fact it is that extra effort after that point that will make someone a true expert in their field.

Grandpa also encouraged me to speak with other magicians, to watch DVDs and read books on magic. He explained to me the "Razor's Edge" concept. He pointed out that it is sometimes the little subtle things that separate the stars from the rest of the crowd. Many times the difference is as fine as a "Razor's Edge," and that if I did the little things like a master, then the rest would follow.

Grandpa's suggestions have already helped me improve and I know that they will help me in other areas throughout my life.

Making Music

CURTIS PROCTOR
—Grandson (Age 14)

I love music and really like the guitar. An uncle of mine plays in a band, and had been encouraging me to learn to play. He knew how much I liked it. I guess my parents knew too, because one Christmas morning a couple of years ago I woke up to find a black electric guitar and amplifier under the Christmas tree! It felt amazing to hold. I was so excited—I was going to be a rock star!

I started to take lessons. Soon, I was frustrated—I wasn't making music, I was making noise. It was a lot more difficult than I thought it would be. I couldn't even get my fingers to bend over the strings properly. I was discouraged and didn't practice as much as I should have.

But I persisted with my lessons. Very slowly, I started to make some basic sounds. It still wasn't music, but I started to think there was a chance I might actually be able to play something ... someday. I started to practice a little more, but it wasn't as much fun as I had hoped. I even considered giving up.

The more I attended my lessons, the more the right sounds started to come. I started to practice even more. The better I got, the more I practiced and the more I started to enjoy it!

One day while visiting with Grandpa, he was talking about goals. I don't even remember who he was speaking with, but I remember one comment he made that day. "Success is a journey, not a destination."

I thought about my guitar and all the guitar players that I wanted to be like. I realized at that moment that there is no destination in learning how to play the guitar. You can always get better no matter how good you are. Learning to play the guitar is a journey. It is the learning that has to be enjoyed. There is no alternative if there is no destination.

From that day forward I never looked at my guitar lessons the same way again. I stopped focusing on the player I wasn't and started enjoying the small successes I was having each time I practiced. I now play my guitar every day and constantly focus on improving and enjoying making music. I am in my second band and look forward to the day when I perform in front of a live audience. If Grandpa hadn't said those few short words I would likely still be focused on the destination rather than enjoying the journey.

Bob's Daughter

MICHAEL FILICETTI
—Son-in-law

From the time Colleen was a little girl, dance was her passion; in university that was her major. Following school she danced professionally for a period of time, even traveling internationally. She and I met just as she had finished dancing and as she was finding her way in the business world.

As with her dance she was very conscientious and industrious in her work. She not only had a primary job, but took on other part time work and projects. She was pretty, talented and driven. We clicked immediately on many levels.

Ultimately we married and when we started our family, Colleen made a decision to throw all of her time and talents into being a full time mother to our four children.

I watch Colleen's patient and positive attitude in raising our children. I fully appreciate her ability to "keep the main thing, the main thing"—her family. I have known Bob for over 25 years and those same qualities that I admire in Colleen....I clearly see in Bob. I realize now how fortunate I am to have Bob as my father-in-law, and my children's grandfather. The lessons he taught Colleen are the lessons my children and I are all benefiting from. It's a reminder to all parents—children emulate the way you behave and think, from a young age. What are your actions teaching your children?

Do What Is Required

JOHN BRINDLEY
—Brother-in-law

I first met Bob and the family when I was dating his sister Helen. I immediately liked his mother, Marguerite, and Helen's brother, Allan. I felt connected right away. It took a little longer to connect with Bob.

Even at that young age, Bob was the member of the family who was always looking on the other side of the fence. Without permission from his mother, and at the age of 17, Bob joined the Canadian navy. While Bob was in the navy, Helen and I got married.

Bob has never tried to take the easy path in anything he did, nor has he expected any help. When he sets out to do something, he is always prepared to go it alone—never waiting for someone to help or save him.

Bob surprised everyone when he came home for our wedding. What he never mentioned to anyone at the time was that he couldn't really afford to travel back to his ship in Halifax after the wedding in Toronto.

Soon after the ceremony ended, Bob set out for Halifax—hitch-hiking, with just a chocolate bar in his pocket. Without money for food, and nowhere to stay, he spent the first night on the road sheltered from the rain in a phone booth in Quebec.

Bob didn't let his circumstances prevent him from attending his sister's wedding. He never whined about it, nor did he expect financial help. He did what he had to do to be at the wedding, and return to his ship.

Bob's tenacity to achieve what he wants has never let up. He chooses to control his circumstances; he doesn't let his circumstances control him. Watching Bob's dedication to his objectives, I've learned first hand the depth of what he means when he says, "Don't let anything sway you from your goal."

How many times have you abandoned a project because you lacked the help or support you thought you required?

Finding My Purpos

LINDA PROCTOR
—Wife

Summers in Toronto can be beautiful but short. So Bob and I take full advantage of our backyard during this time of year. Bob will set up his computer on the patio table to work; most of his meetings are held right there in the warm sun.

Years ago, during one of these wonderful summers, Bob and I were both at the patio table, working. All right—I was reading and Bob was working. During a break, our conversation turned to having a purpose in life. I admitted I wasn't sure if I knew my purpose.

Bob defines having a life's purpose in simple terms: why you get out of bed each day. What drives you? Bob clearly has a purpose; he fulfills it every day, in everything he does. In fact, when new opportunities present themselves, his first question is, 'Will it help me fulfill my purpose or will it take me in another direction?' If it doesn't fit his purpose, it may still be a good idea—but he passes on it.

Bob asked me a series of questions: What did I like to do? What was I good at? I could think of a number of ways to answer those questions, but knowing they had to relate to my purpose, I wasn't quite sure what to say. Bob asked a new question: "What are you reading?" I don't recall the specific book, but I do recall it

ook on leadership. Bob said he had noticed that I read a lot
oks on leadership. He asked me why. I said I wanted to be a
ood leader, but that I felt I was lacking in some areas. Ultimately,
Bob pointed out that I read books on leadership because I was in
harmony with leadership—that I loved the idea of leadership, and
suggested that the word "lead" should be a part of my purpose
statement.

With that simple observation, I was on my way to establishing
my purpose statement. When I read my purpose statement today, it
feels just as good as it did those many years ago.

If you are not sure of your purpose—What do you love doing?
What do you love reading? What are you good at?—answering
these questions just may help you find your purpose too!

Between Your Ears

PATTI SHAMBROOK
—Niece

When I was 10 years old, I entered the world of competitive gymnastics. It was a grueling but rewarding life for a child. Being highly competitive with abundant energy, I took to it right away.

Once I started competing, I learned that politics and fierce competitors would become a part of my life. It can be very intimidating to compete against girls who are used to winning, and with judges who are used to awarding the same girls all the first place medals.

I loved the sport, but would often feel incompetent in competition. I really was a late starter, and had a lot of catching up to do. Enter Uncle Bob. I knew what he did, and had learned about being positive and choosing our thoughts and reactions to what happens to us in life. I found it fascinating, and it was during those years that Uncle Bob took a very significant role in my life.

He sat with me for hours, teaching me to imagine going through my routines perfectly, over and over again—something Olympic athletes are trained to do. I learned that this can be even more important than my actual work-outs, because my brain was being trained for perfection.

He asked me what I would like to achieve in the next big competition that was coming up. I said that I would love to win it all, but I couldn't imagine beating the reigning champ.

Uncle Bob explained to me that I didn't need to believe it now, but by writing it out and reading it all throughout the day, I would eventually believe it. So in my 10-year-old handwriting I wrote out that I would win every event and win first all around.

It really seemed like an impossibility when I wrote that goal on the little goal card that he gave me, but I kept it in my pocket, and I read it and felt it all day, reminding me of what I was working toward. I don't know when it happened, but at some point I began believing that it really was a possibility, and it became exciting to imagine it.

Uncle Bob had me not only imagine going through my routines but also seeing my scores come up, the applause and standing on the podium getting my medals.

Well, competition day came around, and I came first on three of the events, second on the fourth, and won first all around, being the first ever to beat the reigning champ.

I only stayed in gymnastics for three years, but the lessons I learned through Uncle Bob marked my life forever. It's risky to believe in things that seem impossible; but it's so much more exciting to go after those goals with belief than to put all that work in and be defeated before you even start because of your negative thoughts.

I am married and the mother of three teenagers now and the training that I received from Uncle Bob has been invaluable.

I went back to university last year to get my master's degree in counseling to be a Marriage and Family Therapist. It's a long road before I am actually licensed, and it's easy to let my thoughts run to all the reasons why I shouldn't have attempted this, and all the

ways I could fail. But I now know that what I choose to
and stay focused on, will happen.

I know Uncle Bob's lessons pertain to all of life. Our thoughts
are everything. A friend of mine likes to say, "All of life goes on
between the ears."

We have a choice in life. We can choose to set our minds on
good and happy things and live more joyful and success-filled lives,
or to think negative, fearful thoughts and be filled with fear and
anger. I know what I choose!

Thanks Uncle Bob!!!

> *"The real issue is not talent as an independent element, but talent in relationship to will, desire, and persistence. Talent without these things vanishes and even modest talent with those characteristics grows."*
>
> —Milton Glaser

Tell Me How You Can

DON PROCTOR
—Cousin

Being Bob's younger cousin, I've had the benefit of his positive affect for most of my life. When I was just a kid, I remember my Dad and uncles driving Fords and Chevys. Bob (still in his 20's) would show up in a new Cadillac. So of course, I wanted to be just like Bob.

When I was 18, Bob invited me to my first seminar. I was wowed—it changed everything about the way I thought! It continues to affect my thinking today. I learned how easy it was to improve the mood of everyone around you by being in a good mood yourself. Bob told me that we create our own emotions with our thoughts. Wake up smiling, and you'll have a good day.

Bob often tells people that to get what you want; you have to do what it takes. I don't believe everyone appreciates the conviction Bob puts into those words. I got a clearer understanding of it myself many years ago. I needed to speak with Bob personally on a matter that was perplexing me. He suggested I come to his office right then and there. It was 7 PM on a Wednesday night, and I had just finished a long busy day; I knew I had another one teed up the next day, too—and I lived a 2-hour drive from Bob's office! I said that I couldn't make it. His immediate response was "Don't tell me why you *can't—tell me how you can*."

I did visit Bob that night, and I'm so glad I did. The conversation was incredibly helpful, and at the end of it, he gave me a copy of Earl Nightingale's book, *This Is Earl Nightingale*, signed by Earl himself! I continue to treasure that book today.

In his seminars Bob talks about the importance of your environment when making changes in your life. When Bob started to study this information and change his life, his new environment consisted of the books he was reading and records to which he was listening. He didn't know anyone who was successful or anyone studying this material. He just kept reading the books and listening to the records over and over…that's how he learned and that's how he changed. Bob put me on a path of reading and studying that I continue today. My life has definitely been enriched by my cousin. Today I enjoy a very successful real estate career and Bob even help me with my first book, *The Secret of Real Estate Revealed*.

He has always given me advice—but more importantly, he's given me hope. The depth of Bob's meaning when he tells people that, *"if they really want something, they have to be prepared to do what it takes"*, has been the most significant piece of advice in my life.Bob walks what he talks.You can't meet demands half way. Bob never has, and he taught me that I couldn't either. I owe much of my success to his positive, can-do teachings and support. As always your biggest fan!

Who's Stealing Your Dream?

ALLAN PROCTOR
—Brother

Back in the late '60s, when he was working at the Nightingale Conant Corporation, Bob had the opportunity to meet many of the inspirational speakers of the time: Dr. Norman Vincent Peale, Charlie "Tremendous" Jones, Og Mandino and Paul Harvey, to name just a few. Bob was a serious student of material on human potential and he read and listened to everything he could get his hands on. These dynamic speakers inspired Bob!

Bob finally reached a point where he was starting to develop a desire to teach what he had learned. He wanted to influence the lives of others, and offer them the opportunity for positive change, just as his own life had been changed. He had settled on a method to help the most people, in the most effective way. He believed people would be impacted by recorded programs if they were first taught the information in person, in a seminar; then used tapes to provide ongoing repetition and reinforcement of the information they learned first hand.

Bob started by recording some of his ideas on a tape recorder (it was a big, bulky reel-to-reel tape recorder—that's how long ago it was!). Bob's first tape was amateurish by his own admission, both in production and content. But it was an important first step. He wanted to share his idea with someone and wanted their support.

So he decided to share his recording with a friend—someone whose opinion he respected.

Bob went to this person's home one night and played his homemade tape. While his friend did not shoot down the idea, he may as well have. Bob said that he could feel through his body language and lack of enthusiasm that he was embarrassed for Bob. Bob didn't know what to say. Humbled, he quickly packed everything up and left.

Doubt had entered his mind. But on the drive home, Bob realized he nearly let that person steal his dream. Bob said that when he realized what was happening, he redoubled his commitment to his goal. This time, he didn't share it with anyone. He just got to work.

The seminars were not a success overnight. Bob worked hard—he kept his vision, of room after room, full of people he could help, until it became a reality.

How many times have you shared an idea with someone, and because of their reaction, you abandoned your dream? Bob tells us that our dreams are our own; ours to create, ours to pursue, and ours to achieve. Believe and achieve!

A Proud Canadian

LINDA PROCTOR
— Wife

Bob is a Canadian—a very proud Canadian. I, on the other hand, hail from south of the border—the United States. This has presented some interesting situations, conversations and debates over the years.

Some time ago, Bob and I travelled to the US to attend a friend's wedding. We flew in the day before, to enjoy the pre-wedding festivities. It's not often that there is absolutely nothing on his schedule on any given morning. So, on this rare occasion, we lingered in bed to fully enjoy the freedom from his hectic schedule.

We were engaged in a quiet conversation, which turned into a debate about our respective countries. Bob was winning the argument until I mentioned to him that I had recently read in a Toronto newspaper that the Canadian Navy had "lost" one of its three submarines in the Great Lakes.

Well, this was just too much for him to overcome, so in his loudest voice possible—and without regard to the other hotel guests—Bob began to sing the Canadian national anthem: O Canada! I tried to stop him, I tried to quiet him down, but he insisted on singing the song, right to the end! I can only imagine what the folks in the surrounding rooms were thinking—we were in Alabama for Pete's sake!

The non-public Bob Proctor not only reads books on self-development, leadership and motivation; he also reads biographies, history, political books and articles. Bob is interested in everything around him and doesn't take any of these things for granted.

One of the lessons Bob frequently teaches is on responsibility, and as I've observed Bob, that applies to all aspects of his life. Being Canadian is much more to Bob than living in Canada and having a Canadian passport. The rights and privileges that come with being Canadian, and living in a free country, are taken very seriously by Bob. When an election nears, he gathers the necessary data to be informed of the issues and the candidates. Armed with these facts, Bob makes his decision and then makes his voice heard: He votes.

Books

BENJAMIN PROCTOR
    —Grandson (Age 12)

Every day I sit down on my bed and read one of the books I have collected. I have close to 100 books, and I keep them in a special bookcase in my room. I believe my love for reading is a gift from Grandpa. Not many kids my age enjoy reading. Most of my friends think it is boring.

Reading is a great and powerful way to get knowledge. I don't think many kids see how many places reading can take you. I have been enjoying reading for about five years. It has helped my grade level at school and I am able to talk about a lot of subjects in class that my friends don't know about.

One day after reading a book about matter for science in Grade 5, I kept asking and answering questions when it seemed like most everyone else didn't know what we were talking about. Reading has allowed me to be more confident in what I know.

My parents laugh when they tell people that I like going to the book store more than the toy store. I like toys, but I really enjoy getting a new book. Grandpa has a room in his house that is just books. It has thousands of books. One day I want to have a room filled with books just like Grandpa.

I always hear Grandpa telling people how much he loves to get books and read. He is always telling people to read a book. My Dad

says I sit just like Grandpa when I read. I like to hear that, because
I think it was Grandpa that first got me interested in reading. I think
I'll always love reading, just like he does.

You Know the Answer

RAYMOND PROCTOR
—Son

Last summer I went to Dad's house for some coaching advice. It was a warm sunny day, and we sat at the patio table beside the pool, where Dad spends most of his time. His yard has been transformed into a garden sanctuary, and it's always a pleasure to experience.

I had a dilemma I was trying to work through, and I was finding it difficult. I had made a pretty big decision to outsource my production operation. I had full expectations that this outsourcing agreement would take the company to the next level. After a few months, the customer complaints were growing. The company I had contracted assured me they were on top of it. But I was concerned, as what they were saying, and what I saw to be happening, told two different stories. I was sharing the details with Dad in order to obtain his advice.

When you discuss matters like this with Dad, he rarely gives you an answer or an opinion. He asks you a lot of questions. He gets a sense of your perspective, and then asks a question that will have you see the same issue from another angle. He really helps you work out your own thoughts.

At the end of our conversation, I asked him what the answer was. He replied "You already know the answer." It hit me crystal clear. I did know the answer. I had not been listening to my intuition.

The size of the agreement, and my hope that the original plan would work, was preventing me from focusing on my gut feeling. I decided then and there to act on my intuition and bring production back in house. It did not take long before the service complaints declined and positive feedback started to make its way in.

Not long after this meeting with Dad, one of my managers was in a dilemma of choosing between two people to hire for one position. One candidate was more experienced and qualified for the position—and we needed experience. But the candidate wouldn't be able to work in the office, and we knew the results of working with a virtual operation had proven to be less effective on productivity.

The second candidate was able to work in the office, but had less experience. This person had excellent energy, and the type of attitude we were looking for. My manager couldn't make a decision, and came to me for direction. I immediately thought of my meeting with Dad. I asked a few questions, and said "You already know the answer." She smiled and said, "You're right, I do." I have no doubt that her decision was the correct one.

You know that you have learned an important lesson when you find yourself applying it and sharing it successfully with others.

Go, Brian!

BRIAN PROCTOR
—Grandson (Age 10)

I play hockey in the winter. I normally play defense, but sometimes I get to be the goalie. I really like playing goalie.

I play on a house league team. This is only my second year playing. Most of my teammates have been playing for four or five years. So when I started I had a lot to learn, but my team and coaches really helped me. I try to stop the puck from getting by me no matter what; I often throw myself across the ice to stop it. My Mom calls me the human Zamboni!

The first time I got to play goalie this year, Grandpa and Grandma came out to watch my game. When I skated out onto the ice I heard Grandpa yelling, "Go, Brian!" Boy was he loud; I could hear him so clearly. I felt a little embarrassed, but it made me feel good. He yelled it a few times during the game too. Some of the other players asked me who was yelling my name. I told them it was my Grandpa.

Grandpa yelling my name really got me pumped. I did everything to stop the puck. I blocked almost every shot. I caught them with my glove, stopped them with my mask and sometimes was on my belly knocking the puck away. The cheering got me even more excited. I only let one goal in that game. My team scored six goals!

At the end of the game all the players piled on top of me. I was really proud and happy that Grandpa was there to support me and see my team win. After the game we had lunch with Grandpa and Grandma. My Uncle Brian, Cousin Danny and Gerry Robert were there too. They all congratulated me. Grandpa's support really helped. I hope he can come to more of my games.

Grandpa asked me if I liked hockey. I told him I love it. He told me if I really wanted to, I could play in the NHL when I grow up. But he told me it would take a lot of work. Grandpa told me I could do anything I want, if I put my mind to it.

We won the tournament and finished the year in second place. I'm going to play again next year and practice really hard like Grandpa suggested.

I Think Therefore I Am— Cogito Ergo Sum

PAULA MONCADA
—Cousin

At the tender age of sweet 16, my parents registered our entire family for one of Bob's weekend seminars. I can recall sitting in that seminar wondering why on earth I was there. My parents had dragged me out, (for my own good). I had no interest in being there, and I felt very much out of place. Strangely, when Bob began to speak, I felt as though many of the things he was saying were being directed at my family.

I can't say that I listened to all or even most of what he was saying. My mind kept running to important things—like music, fashion, my new school and the friends at my old school (that I missed). That's not to say that I didn't hear anything. I remember Bob asking us, "What is it you want out of life?" He told us to start listing the things that we wanted in our workbooks. I watched as my mother began writing and writing and writing—she just didn't stop! I couldn't believe she could want that much stuff!!

I didn't know what to write. Not that I didn't want a lot of things, but I was pretty insecure in those days, and somehow, the act of writing my desires on paper took more courage than I had.

Fortunately, some of Bob's message did get me thinking. He captured my interest when he spoke out in Latin. He said, "Cogito Ergo Sum," which means, "I think, therefore I am." That statement captured my attention, and got me thinking about all the things that I felt were out of my control. My parents had moved in the middle of the school year, and I was in Grade 9. I was struggling at the new school, and I missed all of my friends.

But I began to entertain a new thought: "If I think I can get better marks, could I?" Really?

I stopped being the "victim" that day, and understood that I am the master of my own destiny. My attitude definitely started to change. My marks began to improve, and I started making some new friends.

At some point soon after Bob's seminar, I began to develop my self-confidence and found that I could go back to the workbook and begin writing all the things that I wanted. I also found that the more I believed in myself, the more my desires became a reality.

The simple exercise of believing in myself started me on the path to success that I enjoy today. I have been able to accomplish many wonderful things and today I am a successful business-woman, happily married with two wonderful children. I teach and encourage my children to believe in themselves, knowing this is the foundation—the necessary beginning—to accomplishing whatever goals they may have.

"8.5 × 3.67"

PAUL, MALA, JAMES, THOMAS, PETER AND JOHN BRINDLEY
—Nephew and family

One of Bob's favorite quotes comes from Earl Nightingale, who said, "Ideas are like slippery fish: unless you gaffe them with the point of a pencil, they're likely to get away." Uncle Bob took this to heart, and always carries a folded sheet of paper in his breast pocket, to catch any ideas or quotes that might come his way.

On a sunny day in April 2008, Uncle Bob drove north, to the small town of Aurora, to the sprawling, century old campus of St. Andrew's College, a prestigious, all-boys school. He was there to speak at the graduating class luncheon (his great-nephew James was graduating), and the school, in return for his time, was making a contribution to the Malawi Project which Thomas, (one of his great-nephews) would be attending that summer.

Uncle Bob arrived early and so had extra time to spend with the family and distribute the presents he brought for his other two great-nephews, Peter and John.

I was excited for my son, and also for being instrumental in having Uncle Bob come to address the boys at this very special event. The grand, dark-paneled dining hall was packed with excited students in full uniform. The headmaster, faculty, teachers and many parents were there. There were long rows of tables, dressed in crisp white linen, and everyone was in formal wear.

The noise level was high, but when Uncle Bob was announced, it became very quiet. With such casual ease and grace he bounced onto the platform to address the students. From his left breast pocket, he pulled out a lined piece of paper that was folded in thirds. His captivating speech that day, originated from the notes on that 8.5 x 11, folded into an 8.5 x 3.67 piece of paper.

I can't remember all that he told those boys. But I do remember him saying, "You don't need to go to school to get a good education." Of course, this has to be relayed in the proper context of what he was telling the graduates. This caused an outburst of laughter and some agreement among the boys

He didn't talk about how and why he carries the folded sheet of paper everywhere he goes, but I knew that this was habitual, and that he rarely goes to sleep at night without capturing something creative or useful on that sheet of paper.

I have begun to carry the same sheet of paper with me. And I remember Uncle Bob and Earl Nightingale when I find myself quickly jotting down an important idea (before it gets away).

Footprints of Touch

BOB AND PATRICIA MCCRARY
—Father-in-law and Mother-in-law

It was a beautiful spring day in New York City in April 2001 when we met Bob and Linda to celebrate her dad's 70th birthday. The weather was gorgeous but cool, except where the sun broke around the buildings. Bob, Linda, her dad and I had just returned to the hotel from sightseeing when we heard a voice call out to us: "Mr. Proctor, Mr. Proctor!"

Bob turned in the direction of the voice to see who was calling his name, when a young woman reached out to him. "Mr. Proctor, I know you don't remember me, but we met at one of your seminars and I just had to share with you how your words changed my life."

"My husband, my family and I will always be grateful to you. Things were really tough for us, but when we returned home from your seminar we put what you taught us that weekend into action. Our lives have been changed forever, and I can't believe I am standing here talking to you now. This is such a wonderful moment; I just had to thank you again."

Bob, in his usual caring way, took time to listen to this very grateful young woman share with him the impact his words had made on her and her family's lives. The four of us could have hurried along through the lobby of the hotel and ignored her call to Bob, but we didn't; and most importantly Bob didn't. He immediately turned to see who was calling out to him and then he stopped and listened. He thanked her for being so gracious and wished her and her family continued success.

Every day we touch people's lives in the things we say, the things we do or don't do; we leave behind a footprint of that touch. For Bob Proctor, the footprints are many and different with each person.

Bob has spent a lifetime encouraging and inspiring people to be the best they can be, not because he says so, but because he instills in them the belief, understanding and motivation to step outside their box of limitations, maybe for the very first time.

On this occasion, we heard once again the impact of his words. This woman's new belief in herself and her abilities helped her stretch further and realize that her future was without limitation. Her desire to share her gratitude with Bob on that day was very heartwarming for us all. In fact, it was quite amazing.

Bob often quotes Wallace D. Wattles in his book *The Science of Getting Rich*, about "leaving others with an impression of increase." In other words, attempt to leave everyone you come in contact with better off from having met you or been around you. His turning to listen to this young woman's appreciation during his personal holiday is evidence that he surely "walks his talk."

It could have been so easy for him to brush this lady off, so as not to interfere with his family time. Imagine the effect that could have had on this grateful young woman and the lasting memory it would have had on something she held so special. It was a little thing but it surely left her with an impression of increase.

Just do the Work, the Money will come

JAN MOIR
—Cousin

More than 12 years ago, I took a giant leap of faith. I had been working for someone else and applying my talents, only to watch others make a considerable amount of money more than me. I asked myself if I was just comfortable with the safety net of a steady income, or if I had the guts to resign and start my own company.

I recalled words that Bob had spoken: "Just do the work, the money will come." They made sense, yet to be honest, I didn't really believe him. But I knew that I was running out of time to fulfill a lifelong dream of having my own business. I knew that I doubted what Bob told me, because in fact, I feared the unknown... plus all I could focus on was IF I would be able to earn the amount of money I needed to live.

So I applied those eight words from Bob. "Just do the work, the money will come." Bob had a tremendous track record, and he had helped so many others realize their dreams...so I decided to take the risk on whether his words would come true.

I quit that firm and established my own company, in the same field, with a mere $5,000 and some office space from a friend. My regular income was now gone. I was on my own and if I were to make money, it would be entirely up to me. I knew the first three to six months in the start-up phase would be difficult. Not only would I have to make many decisions, I would be putting out money, and not bringing any in.

Bob also told me that I had to do everything I could think of that were results-producing activities. I stepped out and performed every task that needed to be done—no task was too large or too small. They weren't all easy of course, but I knew they had to be done, in order for me to succeed.

When the going got tough, I visualized Bob talking to me. I took that leap of faith, I trusted in Bob's words, and I realized my dream.

Just do the work and the money will come! It works—trust me!

It's Only Stuff

BETH BROUDY
—Sister-in-law

Many years ago after deciding to end my marriage, I turned to my oldest sister Linda and her husband Bob. Being the nurturing and supportive people that they both are, they welcomed my daughter and me into their home during my transition time.

Back then, I was living in Colorado, so my middle sister Pixie, helped me pack up. Together we drove all the way to Bob and Linda's home in Toronto. Looking back, I'm sure Bob had no idea what the next several months would bring, but he sure was a terrific sport.

Soon after I arrived in Toronto, I felt that I needed to return to Colorado to go through personal belongings and furniture and arrange to place them in storage. Bob urged me not to go, saying "It's only stuff, you can replace it." I know that he was worried that I might not be strong enough to endure the emotional turmoil, and that I might even second guess my actions, and possibly return to an unhappy marriage. I did go back, but I also did go through with the divorce, and I was able to stay focused, because I had found a new inner strength that came from being surrounded by my family.

Bob was extremely patient during this time, enduring many hours of sister bonding and obnoxious laughter. He didn't get mad when during conference calls he was forced into the bathroom to clap for my daughter, because she was potty training. Bob and Linda provided a nurturing atmosphere where I was able to heal and find my way back, and that journey was far greater than I ever could have imagined when I first started out from Colorado to Toronto.

I also realize now, that initially my focus was greatly misplaced on the "stuff." I truly was fixated on getting my share. Bob knew that furniture and tangible objects are not what define us. It's what we believe and who we are in our hearts and mind. Nothing could have taught me that lesson better, than living with Bob and Linda.

The Money Jar

BRIAN PROCTOR
 —Grandson (Age 10)

One day when I was over at my Grandpa's house, he asked me to go into the kitchen. We sat down at the table and he brought over a jar of coins that he keeps on the counter. Every time that Grandpa comes home, he empties the coins from his pocket and puts them in the jar. When the jar gets full, Grandpa gives it to one of his grandkids. Everyone gets a turn, and today was my turn!

I was excited! He opened the jar and poured all the coins out in front of me. Grandpa said, "It's your turn, the money in the jar is yours. Let's count it." He helped me sort the coins. It was a really nice surprise, to get the jar that day. I didn't know it was my turn, and it made me happy. Grandpa said he used to do it with my Dad, his brother and sister and their cousins.

While we counted the money, Grandpa told me that money is meant to be used. He also told me that I should love people and use money and not to love money and use people. Grandpa told me to use the money however I wanted.

My Dad was with us and he told me that when they were kids, his cousin TJ bought golf lessons with his jar of money. TJ became a pro golfer and taught other people how to golf.

I will always remember the time Grandpa gave me those coins and told me about loving people and using money.

The Road Trip

COLLEEN FILICETTI
—Daughter

One summer, when I was 14 years old, Dad took Brian, Raymond and me on a road trip from Toronto, Ontario to Fullerton, California. He had just bought a house there, and we were going to spend the summer with him. He told us it was just down the street from our cousin's house, and it had a beautiful back yard with a path that lead to a stable with two horses. I can't speak for my brothers, but I was very excited just to get there, and the thought of a long road trip was not the least bit appealing.

It wasn't the long, boring drive I thought it was going to be, but an entertaining and educational one; as we often deviated from the highway on 'mini adventures'.

Our adventures included watching a parade about the Dalton Brothers in a small town in Kansas; standing at the edge of the meteor crater in Arizona; stopping to see the Petrified Forest; and as my brothers like to remind me, our encounter with a roadrunner, though I would rather forget that one. Along the way, much to my amazement, we actually had a great time. Dad turned that long trip into something very memorable.

Now, when I think back about our road trip, I realize I learned a valuable lesson, though I know that was probably not my father's intention.

I realized as you work toward your goal, it may not always be a straight highway. Sometimes it may take a little longer then planned to get there and that's okay. You may end up on city streets or even a winding country road, but if you keep focused and stay committed, you will get there! I learned to enjoy the diversions, as they are part of the trip and experience.

In reminiscing with my brothers, we all agree that we remember the road trip much more than the vacation.

Today, my husband and I have taken similar trips with our children, making the drive part of our vacation. When they tell Grandpa about their adventures, he smiles and I am sure is thinking about the fun you can have reaching your goal!

And whether he meant it or not, that trip made clear what Dad always teaches: "Success is a journey, not a destination."

How true that is!

Don't Worry Be Happy

DON MOIR
—Uncle

Although I am now retired, my company is still up and running, 35 years after its inception. It's a janitorial maintenance company, which Bob helped me to start.

In the early years, the business operated out of our home. One day Bob was visiting, and I was in a foul mood. I was upset and worried; I believed that I didn't have enough money to cover my payroll. Bob, sensing I was not myself, asked me what was wrong. I explained to him that I was $1,000 short to meet my business obligations.

Bob pulled out a check book, and casually signed one of the checks. Then he handed it to me and said, "Here, use it if you need it." He never asked me how I would re-pay the money. I felt as though the weight of the world had been taken off my shoulders.

A few weeks went by, and Bob came back to visit. When he asked me how things were going, I told him that checks from my accounts had come in, in time to meet my own payroll obligations, so I hadn't needed his check.

As I handed him back his check, he replied, "Well that's good Don, I'm glad to hear that, because there was no money in that account." I still don't know to this day if he was joking. But that statement sure made an impact on me.

Believing I had a safety net because of Bob's check, my attitude and mood shifted; I was allowing everything outside of me, control me. I had been to many of Bob's seminars with my family, but it wasn't until that day that I understood with greater clarity what Bob had been trying to teach me. I realized that I had allowed myself to become a plaything to my circumstances, and that, to take my business to the next level, I would have to take control of my thoughts. I had to be sure never to allow myself to worry over something that may or may not happen, ever again.

Thanks to Bob, I was able to do that. And today, my whole family enjoys the fruits of the business I started so many years ago.

It's a Matter of Perspective

BRIAN PROCTOR
—Son

In his seminars, my father always talks about the Law of Opposites. He says that you can't have a front without a back; an inside without an outside; a right without a left; what is big to one person is small to another, and so on.

I always enjoyed watching the confusion unfold when my father would hold a book up in front of the room and ask someone in the audience if they saw the front or the back of the book. Invariably they would claim they saw the front. My father would insist it was the back and they would always get into a "who is right" scenario. Finally, he would point out that they were both right. The audience could see the front; but for my father, who was holding the book up, he could only see the back.

How frequently do we get so trapped in our own point of view that we actually believe that our way is, the only way—or the best way—when in fact there could very well be better ways out there. I try to remain conscious of that, always searching for different perspectives and staying open to different options.

This "Matter of Perspective," came back to bite me recently. Michele and I were house hunting. We fell in love with one that we both felt was out of our price range. I spoke to my Dad about that home, mentioning that the price was prohibitive. When I told him the price, he surprised me. "That's all?" he asked.

"That's all!?!" With these two short words, Dad caused me to change my perspective. "If that's what you really want then you only need to focus on how you can achieve it." These were Dad's words.

Michele and I had put all our focus on why we couldn't afford the home, and could therefore not see the "how we could." That one conversation with my Dad, reminded me of different perspectives. By focusing on "how we can" we ended up buying the house that we truly wanted.

What The Mind Can Believe, It Can Achieve!

JOHN BRINDLEY
— Brother-in-law

After leaving the Canadian Navy, Bob worked at a series of odd jobs, finally securing employment with the local fire department. It was during this time that Bob's mentor, Ray Stanford, introduced him to *Think and Grow Rich* by Napoleon Hill. Bob read this book over and over. Armed with the inspiration this book provided, Bob left the security of the Fire Department and started a building maintenance business, which became very successful.

At the time, I had been working at IBM in the manufacturing division for over 16 years. I wanted more. Bob said, "Quit your job at IBM and come work with me." Bob made it sound exciting and I felt it might help move me towards the kind of income I wanted, to provide for the things I couldn't have in my current job.

But it sure was scary! I had responsibilities to consider—a young family and a new home. After struggling with this decision for days, I resigned from IBM. I realized that to have the things I wanted for my family, I would have to do something different. Almost everyone thought I was making a huge mistake giving up such a secure position.

Bob virtually guaranteed my success and success for the rest of the staff by starting each day at 7:30 AM with a sales meeting. Before going out to sell our service, Bob always had us focus on our sales goal for the day. Bob helped us to believe that we could reach each and every goal and most often we did.

My decision taught me the value of letting go of status quo in order to pursue my true desires. Letting go became easier when I focused on those objectives and truly believed I could achieve them.

Today my family and I own a very successful business, which in part I owe to Bob with my sincere gratitude.

Focus on the Good

VALERIE FILICETTI
—Granddaughter (Age 11)

Every Tuesday during the summer, my cousins, sisters, brother and I would get together at Grandpa and Grandma Linda's for swimming lessons. We have had so much fun learning to swim and seeing each other.

Of course, learning a new task, such as swimming, can make you frustrated. We would often try a dive and it would turn into a belly flop. Or try a new swim stroke and find we were kicking but not going anywhere.

But we always had one cheerleader at the side of the pool, who encouraged us no matter how many times we failed. That cheerleader was our Grandpa. He never said: "You're doing it all wrong," or "That was a terrible attempt."

Grandpa's words were always kind. "Keep on trying, you're getting it!" Or, "That's great…do it again!"

I have heard Grandpa say that anyone can find fault or criticize a person or situation because there is something wrong with everything and usually it's very obvious. He said that to be successful you must focus on what is right and good which is sometimes more difficult to see.

Grandpa never gives us a negative comment. He is always happy and positive. It is his nonstop encouragement that makes us feel good about ourselves and want to do better.

*"We must walk consciously only part
way toward our goal, and then leap
in the dark to our success."*

—Henry David Thoreau

Goals

CAROLYN HORKINS
—Niece

In the 1960s, when I was in grade school, Uncle Bob's seminar business and his focus on the power of positive thinking were beginning to flourish. Adults were intrigued with the message and the audiences were growing. I was probably the youngest person in the audience and Bob's first school-aged student.

His own children were much younger than me, and I was the only school-aged child in the immediate family that he could teach. Looking back, I think I was the guinea pig, but I was happy to assume the role!

Bob and I fell into a regular pattern. He gave me his books and tapes to read and my parents took me to his seminars on many weekends. At the start of each school year we made a deal. I recorded on a card my goal for the school year. It always had to be over 80%. If I achieved the goal, my prize was lunch at the King Edward Hotel and a new dress from Holt Renfrew's. I always achieved my goal, but of course who wouldn't work hard to realize that prize in June each year! Over lunch, Uncle Bob and I would discuss the goal for the next school year and on it went until I finished Grade 8.

In Grade 8, all students had to participate in a public speaking contest. My topic was "Success." I imagine that the teacher and many of my classmates thought this was an odd topic for a 13-year old, but it was what I grew up thinking about. I won the public speaking contest that year! Of course—it was my goal!

Through Bob and my parents, I have been able to ride the waves in life with happiness and success. I learned as a child how to set goals. With this valuable tool, I worked through the tough times and realized my goal to be a lawyer and later a judge.

Wishing or Being Ready to Receive It!

COLLEEN FILICETTI
—Daughter

When I turned 16, Dad teased me about getting a part-time job. To tell you the truth, I really hadn't thought about a job. At the time, I was a serious student of dance, and I was taking classes several times a week. I had earned my teaching certificate and taught dance classes. Although I wasn't getting paid, I actually thought that I was working!

But Dad had planted a seed.

I took his comment as a challenge. I thought that, if I was going to work somewhere, it would be somewhere that I would enjoy. I decided that I wanted to work as a pharmacy assistant at our local drug store. So later that week, I applied for the job.

When I got home, I told Dad that I had applied for a job. "Where?" he asked. I told him. Then of all things, he asked me where ELSE I had applied. I looked at him, perplexed, and replied, "Nowhere".

He asked if I didn't think I should apply to other places as well. I told him that I wanted to work at the drug store, so it seemed pointless to apply anywhere else. He then asked me if I was only "wishing" for a job or if it was something I was ready to receive.

I was confused. I wasn't sure I knew what he meant.

Dad said there was a difference between wishing for something and being ready to receive it. No one is ready for something until they believe they can acquire it. If I was only wishing for a job, then I hadn't really committed to it, and if that was the case, how would I attract it? But, if I truly desired it, then there is strength in that feeling and in turn dedication to it; ultimately, I would form a commitment to that desire.

I thought about what he said to me; I realized that, initially, when I first applied, I had only been "wishing" for the job. But the more I thought about it, the more I began to realize I really wanted to work there. I liked the people, I liked the atmosphere, I thought it would be really interesting work. I started to visualize working there, and I became excited. I was going to have that job!

You can imagine how excited I was when I got called in for an interview. I have no doubt that it was my enthusiasm and passion that convinced them to hire me. That job has come and gone, but now if I want something, I don't just wish, I become focused on it and truly believe I am ready to receive it.

Energy Plus!

TONI PROCTOR
— Daughter-in-law

Bob will soon be 75. Most people his age are thinking about what time to have their meals, and how they should fill their day. Not Bob. His calendar is jam-packed full of meetings, speaking engagements and travel. For as long as I have known Bob, he has never complained about not having energy, not feeling well, or about how busy he is. What motivates this man?

Bob has always said that when you have a goal and become emotionally involved in it, all that you need will come to you to make it happen. The energy to accomplish your goal is one of those elements.

Recently Bob and Linda celebrated their 25th anniversary. To celebrate, they decided to take Bob's children, Brian, Colleen and Raymond, and their spouses on a 10-day holiday to Paris and Rome. As Bob's daughter-in-law, I was excited to go. We arrived at the airport in Toronto to fly to Rome. As we make our way through the airport Bob is out in front, leading the group. "I'm sure this is because he is familiar with the airport," I told myself. Bob spends a lot of time in airports, travelling the world. The plane lands in Rome, we disembark, and again Bob is out front and all seven of us are trailing behind. We start to laugh, because we can't keep up.

Before we know it we have lost sight of Bob. This scenario became routine on our trip.

Bob carries a goal card in his pocket. Over the years the goals have changed, but the constant factor is that he is always working toward the accomplishment of a worthy ideal. I believe this gives him the energy to accomplish a task that to most would seem impossible.

A missile moving at a fast speed is harder to knock off course than a slower one. It is the momentum that keeps it on course. Bob is in a constant state of deliberate momentum, moving toward his goal. The fact that Bob has always had a goal is a strong contributing factor to his healthy, energetic attitude.

I know that if I want to live a vibrant and rewarding life, I need to always have an objective to work toward, a goal I am so passionate about that it energizes me.

Bob's Angel Food Cake

(Linda's Aunt Julie taught Bob how to make a great Angel Food Cake)

The directions are taken word for word from the paper on which Bob wrote the recipe following Aunt Julie's instructions!

Ingredients:

- 1 ½ cups of egg whites at room temperature (approximately 11 large)
- 1 ¾ cups of sugar (sifted, then measured)
- 1 cup plus 2 tablespoons of cake flour (sifted once then measured)
- ½ teaspoon of salt
- 1 teaspoon of vanilla extract
- 1 teaspoon of almond extract
- ½ teaspoon cream of tartar

Preparation:

Preheat over to 375° F—do not grease pan!

Directions:

Mix at high speed until foamy—Egg Whites, Salt, Vanilla Extract, Almond Extract. Then add Cream of Tartar to the mixture. Continue to mix at high speed until glossy. Fold in 1 cup of the sifted sugar in three equal lots....do not let spoon break the surface of the mixture.

Now add the remaining ¾ cups of sugar and flour in three equal lots (sifted together 5 times)…folding carefully into the mixture. Cut with a knife 11 times.

Cook for 30–35 minutes in a preheated oven at 375° F in a tube pan. Do not grease pans.

Cool upside down for approximately 1 hour.

BOB PROCTOR
Chairman, LifeSuccess Productions

For over forty years my company has focused on all aspects of personal and professional development for corporations and individuals. If you have a desire to improve your business or the quality of your life personally, please visit www.bobproctoreducation.com and discover what we have to offer.

We welcome the opportunity to serve you.

Acknowledgements

What we know about individuals, no matter how rich the details, will never give us the ability to predict how they will behave as a system. Once individuals link together they become something different ... Relationships change us, reveal us, evoke more from us. Only when we join with others do our gifts become visible, even to ourselves.

Unknown

When I suggested that this book be written, every member of the family immediately voiced their willingness to participate. It has been a labor of love; a true collaborative effort. And true to the words in the quote above, we have all learned more about ourselves, each other and of course Bob in this shared pool of information! We are an even closer family because of this book.

Special thanks and hugs to Colleen Filicetti (my rock), Brian Proctor, Raymond Proctor and Toni Proctor for the many joyful hours they devoted to this project and their willingness to endure my relentless re-edits!

Mark Victor Hansen, although extremely busy, you freely accepted to write the foreword. You are a true giving machine and much treasured!

Mike Ashley, Phil Goldfine and John Assaraf thank you for so eagerly sharing, with the world, a small insight into your relationship with Bob and it's impact on your lives!

Maria Morgis and Wendy Gallagher for helping us bring this book to life with your editorial suggestions. This book is better because of your support and efforts.

Lloyd Arbour….your work on this project took it to the next level…thank you so much!

Pixie Low, thank you for being so willing to help with "the work" to complete this book!

Sandy Gallagher–Alford, CEO of LifeSuccess Productions LLC (my husband's company) for your willingness to believe in what we were doing and get behind our efforts!

Gerry Robert, Paul Martinelli, Jim Pallister and Holli Walker thank you so much for your assistance.

Our publisher, Sanjay Burman, you have been a joy to work with through all the processes of getting this book to market. Thank you Sanjay!

Bob Proctor, the one who "inspired" us, and who continues to inspire us, in the way you live each day! We love you!